THE LONG WAY HOME

Stories of Life Beyond Goat Pasture Road

Susan Swicegood Boswell

Copyright © 2016 Ms. Susan Swicegood Boswell
All rights reserved.

ISBN: 1530495237
ISBN 13: 9781530495238

Edited by Katie Fennell

For my mother, Mary Louise Young Swicegood:
the original
Girl from Goat Pasture Road

For Sally,
Wishing you the greatest of adventures! Friends make the best travelling companions!
♡ Much love,
Susan Swicegood Boswell

TABLE OF CONTENTS

Introduction	vii
Chapter 1: Road Trip	1
Bernie the Pound Cake	2
Steel Mags	5
Pink Catalina	8
Lala Salama	12
Chapter 2: Alternate Routes	17
Prize Heifer	18
Fortune-Teller	23
Shoe Whore	26
When God Meets Rocky and Bullwinkle	30
Chapter 3: Highway One	33
Reduction Cooking	34
BIG LOVE	37
Empty Nest	40
Tapestry	42
Chapter 4: Flat Tire	44
Ballerina	45
I'm All Out of Pluck	51

$100 Hair Spray	54
The Spies Next Door	57
Chapter 5: Traveling Light	61
Hailing a Yellow Taxi	62
Churchland Baptist	65
Etiquette of Dying	68
Sea of Dreams	73
Angel Band	77
Chapter 6: Over the River, Through the Wood	82
The Christmas Tree	83
The Gift of Real	86
Shine On	90
The Piano Bench	93
MIA	97
Chapter 7: U-turn	100
Toudie's House	101
Hitting the Mark	105
Treasures in the Attic	109
Incarcerated	114
Fearless	118
Resurrection	121
Epilogue: Glimmer	123
Acknowledgments	147
About the Author	149

INTRODUCTION

For most of my life, I have taken the long way home. While I may occasionally make the choice to dawdle or to meander along the back roads for the simple pleasure of a scenic route, taking the long way home has been more often the result of a happy accident. The truth is that I am forever getting lost. Just ask my husband, Perry; he'll tell you. He will say that when it comes to knowing where I am going, I couldn't beat my way out of a paper sack if my life depended on it. My internal GPS is such a mess that when the two of us go out for a drive and are not certain which way to go, he'll ask my opinion and do just the opposite.

Over the years, I've come to view my skewed sense of direction as something of a gift. With me at his side, I figure my husband will never need to spend another dime on road maps.

Now I realize that not everyone out there shares my navigational philosophy. I have a theory that these are the kinds of people who are never late for appointments. They never run out of clean socks and underwear. They keep casseroles in their freezer, alphabetized by type and cross-referenced by date of expiration. Their lives operate like a well-greased engine, efficiently humming along the highway of life like a Toyota Prius.

If this is you, I secretly envy you, but will invariably wonder if you are having any fun.

I drive a beat-up Dodge. It made a horrendous clunking noise yesterday and is currently in the shop awaiting diagnosis. I am not proud to admit it but I often run behind. If I am behind with the laundry and out of clean socks and underwear, I have occasionally been known to wear them inside out. I am not especially fond of casseroles, nor do I do much advance meal preparation. (This leaves plenty of room in my freezer for ice cream.) One of my great joys in life is a road trip. There is nothing more exciting than having my bags packed, a tank full of gas, and the thrill of knowing that there is nothing between me and the open road except opportunity and adventure.

For me, taking the long way home has come to mean acknowledging that our journeys are less about reaching the destination and more about lessons learned on the road getting there. Consequently, journeys change our lives.

In February of 2001, I took one such journey. I boarded a plane bound for Ft. Lauderdale with my friends Angela, Lucia, and Phyllis. We left our worries, along with our families and winter coats, back home in North Carolina. We were in search of some serious girl-time R&R, our own spring break. During a layover in Atlanta, we found ourselves in the Peach Bar and Grill, sipping fuzzy navels from obscenely large tumblers and giggling like teenagers. We became so relaxed that we almost failed to notice that the departure for our connecting flight was imminent. Angela and Lucia hurried ahead while Phyllis and I settled the check and drained the last drops of peach schnapps and orange juice from the bottom of our glasses. As we ambled out of the bar, we could hear Angela — our proper little Southern bell — at the other end of the concourse, screaming from the top of her lungs: "Ru-uu-nnnn!" Her voice boomed like a loudspeaker, echoing from one end of the terminal to the other and back again. I feared there had been some sort of an altercation and that she was single-handedly holding the plane. To the theme song of *Chariots of Fire*, the pedestrians parted as Phyllis and I raced to the plane in slow motion with our carry-ons blazing behind us.

Having averted disaster, we arrived safely in Ft. Lauderdale and rented a forest green Mustang convertible. Our destination? Key West. We skirted the Everglades, coasting down Highway 1 through Key Largo, Islamorada, and Marathon. We stopped at a roadside diner beneath Seven Mile Bridge for the best key lime pie I have ever tasted, before or since. In Key West, we settled into our little B&B off of Duval Street. We set about exploring the town, immersing ourselves in the numerous delightful, cultural eccentricities that define Key West: Ernest Hemingway, six-toed cats, magical banyan trees, soft-shell crabs, drag queens, boys in the band, and rogue chickens.

It was a magical trip.

On the evening before we were to head home, we took a sunset cruise on a wooden schooner, setting our feet back on the shore with all of the giddiness of the complimentary wine and rolling sea still upon us. Strolling along the bustling waterfront at Mallory Square, we danced salsa with the locals. We donned funny hats in the gift shops and perused the aisles for crafts and souvenirs. On impulse, we even sought out a psychic whom Phyllis remembered encountering on a previous trip.

Somehow, among all the street vendors and entertainers, we found Mary. Unlike the other exotic-looking fortune tellers who hawked at us from the boardwalk, Mary sat off to the side, a modest older lady in a plain cotton dress and cardigan. She looked less like a psychic and more like a benevolent grandmother. While Mary professed to have the ability to see into the future, I could only surmise that she must do it with one good eye; I couldn't help but notice the irony. One of Mary's eyes was a well of clear bottomless blue while the other was clouded an opaque milky white; her appearance reminded me of my Grandma Young, who wore a single prosthetic glass eye after she lost her real one to cancer.

We all took turns having our fortune read. While I sat across from Mary on a little wooden stool, Phyllis listened and took notes so that later, I could remember what was said. Mary held my hands lightly in hers and proceeded to tell me about myself. Initially, I was not particularly impressed with her reading; some parts seemed so generalized that they could have been true for most anyone, and other parts simply didn't ring true.

Honestly, I couldn't have cared less about having my own fortune read; my most intimate concern was to inquire about my father. "He is *so happy* that you have asked about him," Mary exclaimed, her face radiating an otherworldly joy even as that clouded eye drifted off course about 10 degrees.

My father was happy! There were no other words that Mary could have spoken that would have filled me with more joy. Eight years before, my kind and much-loved father had committed suicide. He had been severely depressed for more than a year following his retirement. I could not imagine the anguish he must have experienced near the end of his life, and I had lived with the regret that somehow, we had all failed him in the end. Although I was never thoroughly convinced that Mary's skills were legitimate, her words brought me comfort that his spirit was no longer suffering and a certain amount of relief that his earthly troubles had not followed him into the next world. I will always remember daddy's laughter, his gentle sense of humor and the sound of him whistling when he was working around the house. Mary's words helped lighten the burden of grief that I still carried from my father's suicide and let me imagine him joyful, once again.

Fast-forward nearly a decade. Along with the arrival of my middle-age brain fog and hot flashes came a season of unrest. I was busy: I had a teenage son, a mother in the early stages of dementia, a solid marriage to my college sweetheart, and a fulfilling career as an interior designer. Still, I was restless. Each day seemed to bleed into the next. I had always stuck to my life plan: college, career, marriage, motherhood. Now, looking toward my future, there was no sense of excitement, no sense of "what's next."

Then, a strange thing happened. One day, I simply started writing and found that I couldn't stop. At first I journaled, writing about my everyday life — its ups and downs — and about my friends and family. Upon reflection, I discovered that the ordinary became the extraordinary. Taking the jumble of thoughts swirling in my head and putting pen to paper felt as natural as breathing, as calming as prayer. Somehow (and no one was more surprised than I was), I accidentally became an author, joining a vibrant group of women writers within the blogging community of *Skirt! Magazine* and subsequently establishing my own blog, *Girl from Goat Pasture Road*.

And yet a part of me felt silly. Me, an author? I dismissed it as bogus, a fluke.

One evening, over a few glasses of wine, I confessed these doubts to my longtime friend and fellow Key West traveler, Phyllis. I've likely whined away several years of my life on Phyllis's lovely back porch, lamenting this or that, wailing and gnashing my teeth. Phyllis never fails to fulfill the roles of listener, wise counsel, and supportive friend. That night, after she patiently heard me out, she proceeded to blow my mind. "But Susan, you *are* a writer. You were always meant to be a writer. Don't you remember?"

I didn't.

She reminded me of that night long ago in Florida and of the words of prophesy from the fortune-teller that I'd been so quick to dismiss. Until Phyllis located and produced for my inspection the notes she had penned on my behalf that night in Key West, I had completely forgotten Mary's words. Now, holding that relic of thin, crumpled paper in my hands, I could see where Phyllis had scribbled a note at the top of the page nearly a decade ago.

It said, "You are a writer."

I had to laugh. Out loud. My passion — and purpose in life — had found me. I understood right then that in some sense, I had arrived home. *Yes, the long way home, but still home.*

Today, the home of my childhood on Goat Pasture Road, in the wild country of Davidson County, is gone. My parents, aunts and uncles, my grandparents, are all deceased. Ironically, for years, I wanted to leave so much of that place behind me; now that it is no longer there, at least in the physical sense, I long for home. My experiences along the way — getting lost, being found and getting lost again — have taught me that home is an infinite place. It does not exist in isolation, for it is a living place that holds us like breath itself, waxing and waning. We draw near it and push away. We forget and then remember.

That is the long way home. Our journeys, if we let them, will take us there.

CHAPTER 1
ROAD TRIP

"What you've done becomes the judge of what you're going to do — especially in other people's minds. When you're traveling, you are what you are right there and then. People don't have your past to hold against you. No yesterdays on the road."

—William Least Heat-Moon, *Blue Highways*

BERNIE THE POUND CAKE

www.skirt.com/susan-boswell – May 8, 2010
88.5 WFDD, "Real People, Real Stories" – June 4, 2012

In her later years, my mother's cooking went from bad to worse. She boiled green beans until they were devoid of all texture and then seasoned them with saccharin. From pork shoulder to turkey breast, all meats prepared by my mother's loving hands bore similarly dull brown interiors and incinerated skin. Since we were never certain of the meat's biological origin, we simply called all of them "Roast Beast." Even mama's iced tea tasted burned.

Her recipe for a plain yellow sheet cake with boiled caramel icing became legendary at family gatherings and holiday meals. As the icing cooled, it transformed from a smooth, buttery concoction into a wrinkled glob that could be peeled off the cake in a single slab. If pulled slowly and carefully, it could be manipulated like Silly Putty to look like Joan Rivers.

To ensure the safety of our loved ones against the accidental ingestion of the caramel carcinogens, some unscrupulous members of our family developed a secret code that signaled the arrival of this cake at the holiday table. Holding our hands just beneath our noses, we waved them up and down like the trunk of an elephant. From anywhere across the room we could soundlessly shout the alarm, "Beware the elephant skin cake!"

After mother was diagnosed with lung cancer in her late 70s, my sister Janie and I decided to take her away on a long weekend trip to the mountains. Imagine our surprise when we arrived at mama's house to discover that she had made a special pound cake just for our trip. Freshly prepared and thoroughly baked, it was all snug and bundled into her 30-year-old yellowed Tupperware cake container with the removable snap-on lid. Janie and I eyed the cake suspiciously. "Oh no," we thought simultaneously. "Not a pound cake!"

If you have ever seen the movie *Weekend at Bernie's*, you can imagine what it was like to go around with a lifeless cake for a traveling companion. In the cinematic version, "Bernie" was actually a dead body that was transported by two harebrained guys to all sorts of events. Behind dark glasses, Bernie attended a cocktail party. He took a boat ride. He sunbathed at the beach.

Such was the story of "Bernie the Pound Cake." While we cruised Skyline Drive along the crest of the Blue Ridge Mountains and the Shenandoah National Park, Bernie sat in the back with mama. He shopped for apples and crafts at the local produce stands. He visited Natural Bridge and Monticello. He accompanied us everywhere: into our hotel rooms at night and to every roadside picnic. In order to not hurt mama's feelings, we pretended to be simply too full for dessert.

All went well until we arrived at the Holiday Inn in Charlottesville, Virginia. As I opened the SUV's hatchback to unload our luggage, I could see the Tupperware container scattered among my sister's numerous suitcases and tote bags. I had grown weary of lugging Bernie around everywhere and so I pretended to push him aside in order to reach the other baggage. My sister noticed my sleight of hand. "Oh let's take the cake inside," she said brightly, giving me a wink.

"Are you trying to kill us?" I uttered, my mouth frozen into an artificial smile.

That was the moment Bernie the Pound Cake sprang to life! No more sitting on the sidelines. No more viewing life from behind a nicotine-stained plastic prison. "I want to be free!" exclaimed Bernie. And so he was.

The instant my hand brushed the container, there was an explosion of sorts from the freshness-guaranteed seal. Bernie made a run for it, or shall I say a roll? Landing on his side a few feet from the car, he did the 100-yard dash through the parking lot like a runaway tire, gaining momentum with each curve.

I chased Bernie for about 100 yards before I had to stop, doubled over, my legs pressed together to keep me from wetting my pants. Tourists standing nearby, getting ready to board their tour bus, were laughing and pointing. In my peripheral vision, I saw Bernie almost take down the bellman and a couple of Harleys as he careened down the driveway before landing at the bottom of the hill.

I finally regained enough of my composure to rescue poor Bernie. What an undignified end to our faithful travel companion. He had reached the end of the road, listing on his side in a ditch that was littered with fast-food wrappers and empty soda bottles. Upon closer inspection, however, I could not believe my eyes. Despite his rough and tumble journey across the parking lot, Bernie was miraculously intact. Not an inch of his thick, char-broiled skin had been damaged.

I carried Bernie up the hill and held him out to my mom and sister like an infant for blessing. "What the hell are we going to do with this now?" I pleaded.

My sister, always the daughter to put on a good show for mama, took Bernie from my hands. After giving him a thorough dusting, she popped him back into the Tupperware container. With a light pressure on the lid, Bernie sighed with relief, happy to be home once again. Janie plopped him topsy-turvy alongside our other items atop the bellman's cart. "Yummm," my sister purred, beaming her perfect smile at mother. "Let's take this in. I just might want some pound cake after while!"

STEEL MAGS

88.5 WFDD, "Real People, Real Stories" – May 6, 2012
www.girlfromgoatpastureroad.com – July 31, 2015

For years, we kept in touch through Christmas cards. We scribbled our own handwritten notes inside and included the occasional photograph or Christmas letter. Those were the years when life cruised by slowly enough. We lived secure in the cocoon of our mostly untested faith, smug that our lives were on some straight, invisible track. Family photos of that time showed us as attractive young women in our prime, radiant with good health, flanked by the innocent faces of our children and our still-supportive husbands.

The children grew up, the houses grew bigger and we advanced in our careers. In the blink of an eye, 20 years had passed. Enough time for illness to strike, for marriages to dissolve, for families to be broken, for hope to be lost. We didn't know it then, but individually, a kind of shame had set in. Our lives were not as they appeared. No one's dreams had come true. We wondered, each of us from our comfortable middle-class homes, where we had gone wrong and if maybe it wasn't our own fault.

Two summers ago, we reunited for our first girls' weekend in historic Charleston, South Carolina. During those few days, we discovered that in friendship time, 20 years pass like the blink of an eye. I looked into those faces I once knew as well as my own, faces with whom I'd shared countless sleepovers, teenage pranks, broken hearts, and midnight snacks. We confided in each other the challenges and humiliations we had privately (and sometimes publicly) faced during those years without each other's knowing. We recognized the blessings in our struggles. We gave thanks to

God for dreaming bigger dreams for us than we could have ever dreamed for ourselves, and for giving us the strength to go on. We deemed ourselves "Steel Magnolias," an ode to our Southernness and our ability to persevere.

That weekend, we remembered how to be silly again. God, how I'd forgotten to be silly! We splashed in fountains, made mischief, sang, danced, and closed the bars down! We meandered along Charleston's magnificent cobblestone streets and beneath fringed canopies of Spanish moss. We peeked through wrought-iron gates into private courtyards, fragrant with Confederate jasmine, boxwood, and oleander. On the way to their wedding, an elegant couple passed us in a white horse-drawn carriage. *Clip clop, clip clop.* They were so beautiful and the moment held such promise that we spontaneously burst into song, singing a cappella "Goin' to the chapel..." The couple laughed and clapped in delight. Can you believe that they invited us to their reception?

Oh, and we went skinny-dipping. Fifty-year-old bare asses shiny and wrinkled as newborns. Breasts floating on water like jellyfish in the moonlight. "Oh puh-leaze don't let me lose my clothes!"

And laughter. Always laughter, even with the tears.

Before heading home, we took a final walk along those pristine streets and happened to come across a patch of freshly poured concrete. Who cared if someone else had already written in it? I smoothed away that writing as best as I could with a Kleenex and wrote with a stick, "S-T-E-E-L M-A-G-S," because there just wasn't room for "magnolias." A more appropriate name, I suppose, for girls (I mean women) who skinny-dip in the moonlight and crash strangers' weddings.

In a friendship spanning nearly 40 years, we stand as the guardians of each other's innocence and protect that fragile girliness that is too easily lost in this world. Today, we are disproportionately the same as we were then. Older, but wiser. Beautiful, but not young.

We have rediscovered the beauty of friendship. Time taught us not to judge. Today, we view each other's skewed lives and tragic missteps with the compassion given to a baby bird fallen from the nest. We lift each other with a grace and tenderness that can be difficult to bestow on ourselves.

Before heading home to our separate lives, we pause to take refuge from the sweltering heat for a brief libation in one of the city's swanky hotels. From the rooftop garden, we grasp the stems of our champagne flutes and raise them high, bubbles dancing to the surface like laughter. "To the Steel Magnolias!" we say in unison, then someone giggles and we correct ourselves.

"To the Mags!"

PINK CATALINA

www.skirt.com/susan-boswell – July 7, 2012
Greensboro *News & Record*, "Personal Adds: 'Suited Up for a Summer Getaway'" –
July 27, 2012

Throughout my childhood, I can only recall my mother having owned one swimsuit. It was a 1960s hot pink Catalina with boy-cut legs and a built-in bra that made mother's breasts look like inverted snow cones. Dozens of tiny horizontal pleats along the waistline pinched mother's figure into a perfect hourglass, an ingenious tummy-roll hiding feature that makes complete sense to me now that I also have a middle-age muffin top to corral. Rather than being fabricated from the supple form-fitting materials used for today's modern swimwear, mother's swimsuit was constructed out of something more akin to crushed non-biodegradable plastic food containers.

In my mind, the suit retained the exact shape of my mother whether she was wearing it or not.

Every summer, in preparation for our annual Fourth of July trip to North Myrtle Beach, mom would scrounge around the boxes of old hats and shoes high in the top of her closet until she located the pink Catalina. How I teased her for wearing such an ancient style of bathing garment! I always thought my mother was old; she was 36 when I was born. Compared to my friends' younger mothers, she seemed hopelessly old-fashioned.

My best friend Tracy's mom, on the other hand, wore a bikini. Shelby was so hip — I suspect she went topless when none of her kids were around. In fact, if it had not been for Tracy's mom, I would have likely remained completely ignorant of many fundamental things in life, including sex. With the exception of the firsthand knowledge gleaned by observations of animal husbandry on the farm and steamy, stolen episodes of *The Young and The Restless*, I was still waiting on my mother's "sex talk" years after I was married and when she passed away at age 83. Thankfully, I was saved from a life of sexual ignorance when, at age 12, Shelby presented Tracy with a book designed just for girls that explained the whole kit and caboodle. Years before, she had given Tracy's older brother, Troy, a similar version designed for boys. With the book opened between us, we pondered the careful illustrations and scientific terminology but found that it was some time and firsthand experience later that either of us could begin to comprehend some of the book's more ambiguous concepts, such as "orgasm."

Unfortunately, I didn't know then that I would eventually pay many times over for the cruel jokes cast upon my mother and her swimsuit. Karma took me down like one of those rogue waves of the Atlantic. For reasons unknown to me, God saw fit to make me an ugly duckling and my sister, a swan. While I have the natural proportions of a Weeble, my sister enjoys the kind of body that is normally married to NASCAR drivers or can be seen lounging by the pool in one of the *Housewives* shows. Despite the fact that she is 11 years my senior, Janie still wears all sorts of tiny two-piece bathing suits in a dazzling array of exotic colors and patterns. Some have iridescent sequins here and there and are held together by so many tiny bands and buckles, they more accurately resemble orthodontic appliances or tropical fishing lures.

Ever since I became a mother myself and gave up exposing my midriff, my sister has frowned at my sensible choice of tankini swimwear and refuses to even acknowledge my suit as being a two-piece. In addition to being comfortable, my choice of swimwear supports my enjoyment of the beach. I take special delight in frolicking around in the surf and I often emerge from the water looking like a sea monster, although I would prefer that she call me a mermaid. My hair is disheveled where I've been knocked around by the waves and the zinc oxide has smeared from my nose to a host of other places. Inevitably, there is sand in the crotch of my suit where I sat in the shallow pools soaking like a sow in a hog pen.

My sister, meanwhile, emerges refreshed from her dip in the water looking like Venus in a shell surrounded by pearls.

"We need to get you a two-piece this year," she declares staunchly. I swear, it is as if the security of the free world depends on my choice of beach attire. I watch her scrutinize my body for options, trying to envision me in something sparkling and synthetic. "I already own a two-piece," I retort. "All my bathing suits are two-pieced." What does she think I am, a dinosaur? I refuse to be our mother in her pink Catalina! (This is the moment when, in my mind, we have suddenly been cast in a movie. My sister is Heidi Klum and the role of Susan is being played by Melissa McCarthy.) My sister looks both beautiful and confused for a minute, then says dismissively, "No, no ... I mean one with a *real* bathing-suit bottom. The ones that you wear have those long skirts."

She gestures disparagingly and shakes her head at me as if I'm Amish or something.

As if the humiliation I will inevitably suffer appearing beside my sister on the beach is not enough, another mishap recently occurred that can only be attributed to the spiritual workings of my deceased mother. As I began packing my suitcase to spend the Fourth of July with my sister and her family at Ocean Isle Beach, I pulled down the bag from the top of my closet where, just like mom did, I keep swimsuits and other items I access on a limited basis. I ruffled past a stash of tote bags and winter boots until, sure enough, I discovered my old navy blue "skinny" tankini. I immediately tossed it aside for obvious reasons until I found another old navy blue "fat" tankini that had been stretched saggy in the top and skirt. I looked everywhere but I could only find one-half of the suit I was looking for: last year's fashionable and very expensive "medium-size" brown and pink polka-dotted tankini with a short skirt. For some reason, I could find the top but not the coordinating skirted bottom. I looked in the sock drawer, in the drawer with my T-shirts, and in the bottom of the closet among the dust bunnies and leftover plastic shopping bags with tags and receipts that I keep hidden from my husband.

My elusive, somewhat cool, but probably not "cool enough for my sister" swimsuit was nowhere to be found.

They say a good man is hard to find, but if you've ever shopped for a good swimsuit, you know what I'm talking about. From my beach chair in my "fat" navy blue tankini with the skirt down to there, I think how sorry I am for what I said to my mother all those years ago and write in the sand ten-thousand times: "K-A-R-M-A S-U-C-K-S!"

Susan Swicegood Boswell

LALA SALAMA

www.girlfromgoatpastureroad.com – October 23, 2014

The months and weeks leading up to my safari in Tanzania, Africa, were a time of intense planning and preparation. I double- and triple- checked my passport. I reviewed medical records with my doctor to make sure I had been inoculated against all potential diseases. I filled prescriptions to take with me for malaria pills, pain medication, and antibiotics. I procured DEET bug spray and antiseptic wipes and sunscreens with higher numbers than my age. I packed the kinds of smart clothing that would keep me warm during cool nights and evenings and also keep me comfortable when the daytime temperatures inched into the 90s. Even the color of clothing was an important deterrent from the nasty biting tsetse flies. I took various scarves, hats, and handkerchiefs to protect myself and my camera gear from heat and dust. There were electrical converters that would be needed, and chargers for my laptop and cameras. I would even need chargers for charging the other chargers that would allow me to stay out in the bush without my electronics dying for the biggest part of the day. In addition, I packed extra batteries for my camera and even a second camera in the unlikely event that something happened to the first one.

I would be travelling with my sister, Janie. In the months before we were scheduled to leave, there was an outbreak of the Ebola virus throughout the continent of Africa. While there were no recorded incidents in Tanzania, the country we would be visiting, viruses know no borders. We monitored the situation with the CDC and our travel agency until the last minute, making sure it was safe to travel. My son confessed to having a bad feeling about the trip, cautioning me that a "Blood Moon" lunar eclipse was to occur during the time we were in the Serengeti. What felt like a bad omen to him felt like high drama to me. I could hardly wait to see a crazy orange moon floating over the African savannah.

While in Tanzania, one of the most beautiful in the handful of words I learned to say in Swahili was "lala salama." This expression means something akin to "have a safe and peaceful night's rest." Isn't that a beautiful way to say good night?

We were prepared to see all kinds of African wildlife on safari and we were not disappointed. In addition to the Big 5 (elephants, rhinoceroses, lions, water buffalo, and leopards), we saw amazing birds and smaller mammals as well as incredible specimens of trees and plant life that had found unique ways to adapt and survive in the harsh environment.

What I had not anticipated, however, was how magical the evenings would be. In the Serengeti, the land is mostly flat and the sky seems to go on forever. Every evening at dusk, I tried in vain to photograph the moment the sun touched the horizon, but it slipped away, melting into a streak of fire with an expansive afterglow. Interspersed among the grassy plains are low mountains topped with any number of species of sparse acacia trees that, when silhouetted, appear exactly like unruly elephants marching across the peaks. I loved sitting around the campfire and rehashing the day's events.

The light illuminated the faces of our group and of our leader, Zablon Sunday, but did not extend to the darkness beyond us, where things would occasionally go bump in the night. Amorphous shapes flew and fluttered across the sky; moths and bats dove for their dinner. The beam of a flashlight could catch the glowing red eyes of hyenas in our new front yard. One of my favorite sounds at night was their piercing call of *woo-OOH*, one of five distinctive calls that they make along with their trademark "laugh," which Zablon seemed to think sounded a lot like me. The campfire was such a fitting and relaxing end to the memorable days spent in nature, that it had the effect of a prayer.

On our first evening in the Serengeti, Janie and I returned to our tents after dinner to find our neighbors Shirley and Helen dancing in circles, worshipping the sky. Here in Sub-Saharan Africa, these ladies were not doing a native dance. On the contrary. Modern technology had found us again and they were busy identifying constellations with their iPhones. The sky was magnificent with millions of stars and innumerable constellations. The Milky Way had spilled its contents across the heavens in a huge streak of cream.

No blood, no moon, no Blood Moon, just a glorious evening sky as our Creator meant for it to be. Lala salama!

In the days before we reached the Serengeti, we lodged in a tented cabin on a barren saltwater lake in the area of Lake Burunge. On our first night there, I awoke to hear a loud crunching noise on the other side of the thin canvas right above my head. "Janie!" I whispered. "Wake up!" Sis was slumbering peacefully, oblivious to the midnight snacking of our uninvited guest. I got up from my cot and began stumbling around the tent, trying to locate the flashlight and my glasses. My stirring must have alarmed the creature and I could feel the earth shaking as it raced to the front of the tent. I was unable to see anything through the mesh zipper windows, so I unzipped the canvas door a few inches and peered outside.

In our front yard was a magnificent zebra. He was only five or six yards away, shaking his head and staring at me in disgust. I do not remember having located the flashlight but I recall that he was illuminated — perhaps by the moon — the white of his stripes painted clearly against black. He seemed huge, powerful, and I was utterly spellbound. The moment was so alive that I could see the dust particles moving in and out of his nostrils when he breathed.

I looked around carefully, I really did, before stepping gingerly outside on the porch.

The next day, my sister told Zablon on me and I got in trouble.

⊷⊷

Here in the Serengeti, however, I do not unzip the tent at night and I do not go outside. Upon arrival, our guides gave us a whistle to blow should we become truly alarmed or endangered. It is not safe to go outside during the evening without an escort for any reason other than suicide. At night, even when I hear what I know is a warthog grunting around the tents, I do not go outside.

There is a small river not far from our campsite and the hippos like to wallow in the nearby brush throughout the night before returning to the pools in the early morning. It sounds as if moving to and from their watering hole is simply too much for them to bear. Our friend Jackie describes them perfectly as "sighing in the key of James Earl Jones." The lions fill in the lower range of sounds with a vibrato that is so low you can feel it. For the last few mornings, as we have driven out of the campsite, we passed by a pair of lions sleeping on the warm earth in the middle of the road. At bedtime, we lie on our cots and hear them roar as they begin their evening hunt. They are the king and queen of the jungle, and the sound that floats across the stillness of the savannah plainly establishes that. The sound is not so close to us that I am afraid; it is simply beautiful, powerful, and comforting the way things are when you are one with the majesty of God's work and the natural order of life.

I also do not unzip the tent on another night when I hear what sounds like a stampede outside. You'd think by this time that I would have given up trying to see out of a mesh window into the darkness, but I have not. I do not know what time it is, but the moon has risen high enough that I can see shadows moving across Helen and Shirley's tent. Just a few feet away, something jumps and kicks up its heels; it moves like a deer. Excitement pulsates through my veins but I retire to my cot and will myself to sleep.

The next morning, Janie and I awake early, before the sunrise. From the other side of our tent, we hear the guides calling softly "jambo," Swahili for "good morning." "Jum-bo," we return, having suitably massacred the word with our Southern accents. The men arrive carrying oil lanterns and pour warm water into the little canvas sink basins outside for us to wash our hands and faces. Suddenly, I remember the activity of the previous night. I locate the flashlight and shine the light into the black void that marks the clearing beyond our tents. We stand there in our pj's, mouths open, to discover hundreds of red eyes staring back at us. We are amazed. It seems the wildebeests stopped by for a little sleepover.

Lala salama, indeed!

A few weeks later, we returned safely from our travels. We avoided contracting malaria and Ebola, and we didn't get eaten by a lion or run over by an angry herd of wildebeests. I've no doubt that all the planning that went into the trip helped ensure our safety and well-being.

Still, there is a part of me that wonders if God doesn't take special delight in planning surprises for his lot of anal-retentive humans. His plans for us are so much more expansive than we could ever imagine. How much energy do we expend on the fears and dramas that plague our minds yet so rarely occur? How blessed are we and how much magic is manifested in our lives when we simply unzip the windows (and sometimes the doors) to our tents and willingly open ourselves to life's next adventure?

Susan dedicates this piece to her "Albu-quirky" neighbors in the tent next door, Helen Feinberg, Shirley Salvi, and the third member of their trio, Nancy Pressley-Naimark. Thank you ladies for a friendship that now spans two continents, includes two husbands, a best friend, a couple of dogs, and some very expensive turquoise jewelry. You gals are the bomb.

CHAPTER 2
ALTERNATE ROUTES

"Just 'cause you got the monkey off your back doesn't mean the circus has left town."

—*George Carlin*

Susan Swicegood Boswell

PRIZE HEIFER

Toastmasters International Humorous Speech Competition –
September 2010
www.girlfromgoatpastureroad.com, "A Touch of Royalty" –
October 9, 2015

There is a palpable excitement that accompanies the arrival of autumn. With a chill in the air, we build campfires and don wooly sweaters. The local Lowe's and Harris Teeter stores stack colorful displays of mums and pumpkins along their curbs. Trees explode into an assortment of magnificent hues, and for a few weeks, no one complains that they will have to rake leaves soon. A kind of routine seeps back into our lives. We set the clocks back an hour and the kids go back to school. Before you know it, it's time for the county fair.

I confess, county fairs make me sentimental. As a country girl, I have always loved wandering through the agricultural exhibits to see who won the blue ribbon for the biggest pumpkin and most delicious apple butter. I enjoy the education areas filled with 4-H exhibits, art displays, and local photography. When I was a teenager, I remember my friends and me riding the Himalaya at full speed to the scream of heavy-metal music as the aroma of fried foods and cotton candy wafted over the midway. Long before anyone thought much about animal rights, we pelted goldfish with ping pong balls and took them home, where they died the next day because no one owned an aquarium.

These days, it is difficult for me to enjoy the fair with the same innocent enthusiasm of my youth. I grow nervous as we approach the livestock arena; the musty smells of freshly tossed hay and animal waste overcome me. My palms begin to sweat and my head

The Long Way Home

feels lighter than normal. That's when my husband begins goading me: "Honey, remember when…"

―――⟨+ +⟩―――

In high school, the senior class was responsible for electing three beauty queens to represent the school in local and community events. The most prestigious queens were the Homecoming Queen and Miss West Davidson.

The Homecoming Queen has always been the stuff of high school legend. Although good looks, poise, and grace are mandatory for any serious Homecoming Queen contender, it helps if she is well-liked and stands out among the other candidates on the ballot. My best friend Tracy Bauernfeind-Jingleheimerschmitz had the longest and most unusual name in the history of homecoming queens. Her name sounded like a Nazi sympathizer and comprised approximately 3/4ths of the ballot's listing. Since her last name started with a "B," Tracy's name was located at the top of the list. Bumfuzzled, our poor classmates became exhausted just trying to pronounce her last name; they marked the ballot with an "x" at the place where they got stuck, and wandered back to study hall. Oh, and did I mention that she was beautiful, sincere, popular without being skanky, and loved by every single person? Still is, even to this day. As Homecoming Queen, Tracy's prizes included a bouquet of red roses, a real tiara, a full-page spread in the yearbook, and an escort by the handsome quarterback.

The second most popular queen was Miss West Davidson. This title came with real distinction, a professionally-printed sash, celebrity appearances, and a genuine cubic zirconia crown barely visible atop her frosted Farrah Fawcett hairdo. This hairstyle was emulated by every girl in 1980. "The Farrah" referred to Farrah Fawcett-Majors, of the *Charlie's Angels* hit television series. Believe it or not, her hairstyle was even more famous than Jennifer Aniston's

"The Rachel" in the 1990s. It was what Kate Gosselin's "Chicken 'do" tried to be a few years ago, although its popularity stint was brief, albeit deranged. "The Farrah" was the ultimate big hair, a wavy, layered cut distinguished by a center part and voluptuous "wings." It didn't matter if your hair was fine and flat as a pancake. With the right home permanent wave, hot rollers, and loads of hair spray, anyone could emulate Charlie's sexiest angel. Miss West Davidson was the most sophisticated, by far, of the three queens. She needed to possess the kind of beauty that could turn both heads and wallets. One of the requirements of the title was that this queen be chauffeured in the various community parades. Any Miss West Davidson worth her salt needed to attract the attention of a distinguished escort beyond our senior class bozos. This job required a man, not a boy, with facial hair and a serious sports car, preferably a black Corvette. Miss West Davidson perched atop the Corvette having already mastered the wave and mortared hard candy on her lowly subjects. Of all the high school hopefuls, only our classmate Lisa Dawn Jacobs possessed this kind of magnetism. The last time I saw her, 20 years after we had said goodbye to our Candie's and shoulder pads, she somehow looked exactly the same yet completely in vogue. We all would have hated her if she wasn't so darned nice.

So what about the third beauty queen?

The last and final beauty queen, our school's representative for Miss Davidson County Fair, received none of these accolades. No Corvette. No tiara. No roses. No quarterback. The least ranking of all the high school beauty queens would vie for the title against the larger and more sophisticated schools in the county. Somehow, our school's representative for 1980 was me.

In retrospect, winning the title of fair queen felt more like winning "Miss Congeniality" than a real beauty contest. I was friends with most of the kids in my class and had known most of them all my life. From the beginning of my life, it was evident that I would not develop into beauty queen material. My disdain for dressing up and my natural lack of elegance and grace continue to be among my most defining characteristics. My husband suggests that my classmates wrote me in because I knew how to plow with a tractor or simply because I retained most of my teeth.

Still, the moment my name was announced over the school's intercom, I felt like Cinderella. Whatever stroke of fate earned me this distinction, I knew it was imperative that I wear the right dress for the big competition against the other girls. This was problematic because I had not actually worn a dress since my fourth-grade piano recital.

My sister Janie made my transformation her pet project. She swore to make a swan out of an awkward and ugly duckling. Since I had yet to develop any sense of personal style, she opted to turn me into her "mini-me," although we look nothing alike. Janie is tall and thin with legs that go on forever. I am more like a Weeble by nature, broad and squatty with legs that appear to be missing at least six inches from the knee-down. Walking on stubs gives me no natural grace. Once when I was a junior bridesmaid in my cousin Patty's wedding, her brother teased me, saying that I walked down the aisle like a linebacker. For the record, I have always been a proud tomboy and hated getting gussied up. On the day my sister and I went shopping for my pageant outfit, she made me try on an endless array of dresses, like in the movie *27 Dresses*. We finally settled on a kind of hippy-looking dark peasant frock that disguised my broad shoulders and supposedly emphasized my best attributes, whatever they might have been.

The judging for the pageant was always held on a Thursday evening, in the same barn and on the same night as the semifinal judging of the cattle and other livestock. This simultaneous timing of events was no coincidence, as it allowed the fair organizers to utilize the same judges for the queens that they used for the Holsteins. Yep, me and Elsie the prize heifer were paraded around the same ring and inspected by the same panel of judges. Elsie was led in wearing her new stiff black halter and I wore the equivalent ensemble, courtesy of J.C. Penney and Dress Barn. When I almost messed my panties because of my nerves, I found comfort in knowing that Elsie had already broken that ground for me.

I made it down the runway in my four-inch heels without falling on my face or randomly tackling the other contestants, but at center stage, I met my waterloo. Who knew that like the real Miss America contest, this contest also included an interview? I had not anticipated having to talk like a spokesmodel in addition to the challenges of simultaneously walking, holding my stomach in and my shoulders back and looking pretty.

Whatever happened center stage that night has been involuntarily blocked from my memory. I do not recall anything that the pageant emcee said or what I did except that I froze. Elsie the cow, standing beside the stage chewing on her cud, must have looked more intelligent than I did. In my dreams, I am still haunted that when I was asked my question, I simply stomped my hoof two times for "yes" and three times for "no."

As an adult, I confess that the trauma of my experience as a former beauty queen has branded me for life. In fact, I had to seek professional help. To overcome my fear of public speaking, I joined Toastmasters. To overcome my fear of fashion, I watched Stacy and Clinton on *What Not to Wear*.

Yet despite my lack of qualifications, I admit I really wanted to win that title, wear the winner's crown, and strut my stuff like a prize heifer on parade. I found refuge, however, that my consolation prize of Purina Dog Chow provided fresh breath while preventing tartar buildup for a long time after the winner's roses had turned to dust.

FORTUNE-TELLER

www.skirt.com/susan-boswell – October 11, 2010

When our old friends Kimberly and Chris decided to throw a big Halloween party for their two boys a few years ago, I was their go-to person to portray the role of the fortune-teller. I eagerly dressed the part, donning a long, flowing skirt, ruffled blouse, and layered all the bling I could find around my neck. I tied a colorful scarf, peasant-style, around my forehead. Dramatic kohl black eyeliner and a long, dark wig masked my blue-eyed blonde. As I gazed into the mirror, I hardly recognized myself. Miraculously, I found my old Ouija board and its plastic controller. A relic from my teenage years, the Ouija board had been a big hit at slumber parties where we had boldly called forth the spirit of Elvis and other long-lost celebrities during impromptu séances. I packed a deck of cards and converted the iridescent gazing ball from my garden into a crystal ball. Voila! My outfit and props were complete.

After the hotdog dinner, I placed my wares inside the tent that had been set up in a dark, remote corner of their big backyard. The wind whispered through the tall pines and oaks as shadows danced across the precision-cut lawn. A candle placed in the middle of the table illuminated my face and that of my young patrons. Miss Susannah was ready for her first customer.

One by one, Kimberly escorted the kids inside. They approached me tentatively, their eyes filled with excitement and apprehension. I played the role to the hilt. When I read the children's palms, everyone had long life lines that showed happy marriages and beautiful children. With dramatic flair, I fanned the cards across the top of the table; a Three of Spades could foretell the same future as the Queen of Hearts. I sprinkled tea leaves into a cup of water where their black amorphous shapes revealed only to me the shape of their future. I gazed into the crystal ball, working in tidbits of information that I had been told about the kids, details about sports or summer camps or their latest crush. It all went off without a hitch until Kimberly brought in my last customer.

At first, I did not recognize the boy. Even when Kimberly said his name, I did not recall anything significant about him. "This is Kyle's friend Ryan," she said. "He and his mom got here late. He'd like to talk to you." "Ah, come in, Ryan," I said with a heavy accent, and motioned for him to have a seat. I read his palm. I sought his fortune in the tea leaves. Unlike the other boys, I could tell my words had failed to impress him. Ryan chewed on his lip; something else was obviously on his mind. "I wanted to ask you about my dad," Ryan whispered softly. Suddenly, I remembered what Kimberly had told me about him.

Ryan's father had passed away suddenly and unexpectedly a few weeks before and Kimberly had not expected Ryan to come to the party. My heart skipped a beat; for a moment, I did not know what to do. Across from me was a vulnerable real-life boy and I was a fake fortune-teller. This child looked at me for some kind of reassurance; I have never felt so small or so embarrassed at perpetuating such a sham. I started to confess, to explain the truth. I wanted to tell him that I was not really a fortune-teller and that I didn't know anything about his dad.

Then I remembered my own experience. It wasn't long ago that I, too, had lost a father. In a chance and singular encounter with a fortune-teller in Key West, I had also asked a stranger about my own father. I hadn't cared so much about the number of children I would have or the length of my lifeline. All I wanted and needed to know in that instant was that my dad was OK.

For a minute, I connected to this boy's pain and told him what I thought he needed to hear. I told him the same types of things that a kind person had told me almost 10 years before. "Oh, Ryan," I began, disregarding my props and my accent and speaking straight from my heart. I told him what I hoped someone would tell my own son should the tables ever be turned. "You know, your father loves you so very much. He is so happy that you have asked about him. I know your heart is heavy and that you miss him. Always remember that even though you don't see him, his spirit is always with you, looking over you and your mom."

I'm not sure if my answer was the right one or if it gave Ryan any comfort. I'm not sure if I should have continued to act the part or if I should have come clean to the poor innocent and injured boy sitting across from me. I hadn't meant to play a cruel joke. I guess I felt that it was important that Ryan believe in something at that moment of feeling so very lost and alone.

Ryan is a grown man now. I've lost track, forgotten to ask about him over the years. Still, I hope he has remembered my words and that he has known the loving and continued presence of his father. I hope, for his sake, that the words of the fortune-teller were true.

Author's Note: As a testament to the inaccuracy of my memory, I recently asked my friend Kimberly Thompson about this story, which I recalled writing just a few years after it happened. When we did the math, I realized that more than a few years had passed between the Halloween party and the writing (and subsequent publication) of this story. Additionally, when I confirmed the details surrounding the death of Ryan's (not his real name) father, I learned that he had passed away years, not weeks, before this party. So much for the accuracy of memory. Additionally, I had forgotten another element of this entire story that was simply too unusual to work into the piece. "Ryan's" father was a landscaper who died unexpectedly while working at the home of my sister Janie and her husband, Gary. I asked her — a week and a half ago to be exact — about the details surrounding that event. She said that on the morning he passed away, neither she nor her husband were at home. They had left their son, my nephew Phillip, sound asleep inside the house, where he remained oblivious to the catastrophic event unfolding just outside his bedroom window.

SHOE WHORE

www.skirt.com/susan-boswell – September 11, 2012

Growing up, my best friend Tracy was tall and I was short. While she stopped just shy of being considered Amazonian in stature and I could hardly be characterized as petite, we were almost identical interpretations of a female Mutt and Jeff. Our contrast in physical appearances undoubtedly led to other contrasts, as well. She dominated in sports, the most perfect teeth, and overall likability by our high school classmates, while I took prizes in creativity and the most memorable Southern accent.

At the beginning of seventh grade, we became fast friends after she moved down the road from me on Goat Pasture Road. I had just traded up from my chestnut-colored Shetland pony, Miss Connie, to a beautiful young Appaloosa mare named Apple. I was anxious to ride the new horse and felt perfectly at ease directing Tracy to ride Miss Connie. It didn't matter to me that Tracy was nearly 6 feet tall and that her legs practically dragged along the ground beside Miss Connie. My excuse? I was spoiled and more than a little rotten. My husband will tell you that I still am.

Despite how unfairly I treated Tracy over the incident with the horses, the only area where we have had an inkling of conflict in our 50 years of friendship revolved around, of all things, our feet. Despite Tracy's clearly superior beauty, I have always pitied her large, flat feet although, admittedly, it would take such feet to keep a 6-foot woman properly upright. We women have our vanities. Some women are proud of their new car. Some are proud of their children. Some want to show off their boob job. Me, I am proud of my feet.

I confess, I am partial to my feet's small, shapely build, their high instep, their little button toesies, and their ability to walk for miles without giving out on me. With regular pedicures and the invention of the PedEgg, I regard my feet as one of my best features.

Tracy has never once given me the satisfaction of conceding that my feet are clearly superior to hers. She's never said, "Gee your feet look nice in those shoes." Or "Susie, I just love that color on your toes!" Instead, over the years, she has stoically crammed those big boats at the end of her legs into an array of flats and sensible sandals while my feet have clearly shined like diamonds.

In our lifetimes, we have weathered our share of ups and downs. We survived raising four children, two husbands, and a myriad of dogs, cats, birds, and goldfish between us, and the deaths of her mother and both of my parents. One of the most difficult ordeals she ever faced was the divorce from her children's father and the aftershocks that rippled throughout her family. Tracy moved through all the stages of grief: from shattered to depressed, afraid to pissed-off, and to what I now consider a healthy feeling of general apathy and disgust for her former spouse (lying cheat). Every relationship requires give and take, but when you are married to a man short in stature and tall in ego with anger management issues, one of those areas of "give" is likely to be in the shoe department. Tracy was married in bare feet, and in all the years she was married, I never saw those big feet of hers clad in anything higher than two-inch heels.

Now, after five years and much harassment from her friends, Tracy has finally begun dating and visiting some popular dating sites. I tease my old friend that she has been single so long that the sexy panties she has been saving to wear have succumbed to dry rot.

A few months ago, another girlfriend and I had a sleepover at Tracy's house. Our intention was to build a huge bonfire and hold a total ex-husband exorcism. The night ended up, however, being not so different from the sleepovers we had so many years ago. The white iron twin bed with the roll-out trundle of our youth was replaced by a king-size pillow top mattress, and the matching pale yellow and purple floral bedspreads had been exchanged for a cozy down comforter. We joked that since Tracy's mother was no longer in the next room, we didn't have to hide the alcohol and listen to her yelling for us to "keep it down." Now, we could be as loud as we wanted.

Still, despite our ages, like any proper sleepover, gossip and chocolate ruled the evening. We sat atop Tracy's bed, strewn with magazines and candy wrappers, as she began to dole out the hidden pleasures of her newly single life. It was one of the first sure signs that my old friend was getting her mojo back. "I have a confession," she began tentatively. For a moment, I was afraid she was going to say that she had sold her soul to pay for health insurance and her kids' cell phone bills. "Now that I'm not married to that Short Angry Little Man (this has become her ex-husband's official name since the divorce), I don't feel like I have to wear flats all the time," she said. "I-I-I'm afraid I have become a shoe whore."

At the revelation of this most intimate secret, Tracy reached into her closet and pulled out box upon box of beautiful high-heel shoes. Some of them had heels so high, I couldn't imagine a foot being able to contort to such an angle. She presented them to me like royalty, in their original boxes, and wrapped in tissue paper. There were bold colors, glistening reds and purples. Patent leathers. Sexy skin prints and barely-there nudes. Such beautiful shoes I had never seen the likes of before. To imagine them gracing her larger-than-life feet was nearly more than I could bear. She stopped short of owning Jimmy Choo's or Louboutin's, but I had no doubt there would be a pair or two in her future.

I purred over each pair. Tracy tried them on and modeled them in her sports bra and pj's. For the first time in our lives, I had to admit that Tracy's feet looked damn good in those shoes. As her friend, I cheered her on. With each slender heel and each bold slit, I knew my friend was going to be OK.

Author's Note: On December 31, 2014, my friend Tracy married the most amazing man, just in time to claim his tax refund and buy — you guessed it — more shoes. Ken is even taller than she is. Thank you, Ken Forster, for making my best friend so happy!

WHEN GOD MEETS ROCKY AND BULLWINKLE

www.skirt.com/susan-boswell – May 14, 2009

We've had a bit of drama this week at the animal house. Nothing contrived, just the natural collision of forces in nature. We have three dogs in our family, including our beautiful Shetland sheepdog, Robbie, who looks like a miniature Lassie. We have another handsome dog, Shredder, who, despite his name, is not a vicious man-eater. He was named by our then-4-year-old son after his favorite *Teenage Mutant Ninja Turtles* character. Shredder is the alpha-male of the bunch, a schnauzer-Australian shepherd mix with a fluffy tail and ears.

Poor Milly, our newest dog, does not exactly share her brothers' good looks. Milly resembles a gargoyle. The vet seems to think that Milly is a mix of rat terrier and Jack Russell. I am not sure how that explains her pea-size head or her bulging eyes or the freckled skin that shows through her thinning coat. Or the wiry hairs that pop up all over her head, lying every which way but down. Or her feet, with their upturned tufts of hair that resemble Dr. Seuss's Grinch or a wocket or a shrew. But bless her heart, what Milly lacks in beauty she more than makes up for in personality. Milly is filled with love and excitement. She wakes up happy every single morning.

While the older dogs pass their days dozing in the cool air-conditioning, Milly braves the heat outdoors. If our veterinarian Dr. Schmunk's best guess as to Milly's breeding is correct, Milly's ancestors were bred to hunt, specifically to hunt and kill large infestations of rats and vermin. Despite the 21st century's Orkin and d-CON, Milly is oblivious to the advantages of chemical warfare. Milly, despite her usual gentle temperament, just wants to be Milly.

The Long Way Home

Two weeks ago, my husband and I discovered an unusual-looking squirrel on the deck, stealing birdseed from the feeder. At the time I first noticed him, I thought he merely looked disheveled and was perhaps missing some fur on his tail. Last week, I found Milly in the backyard barking ferociously. She was pouncing at something on the ground. Fearing that she might have cornered a snake, I rushed to her defense, bearing a flat garden shovel. What I discovered, instead, was that Milly had cornered that poor maimed and battered squirrel! After screaming hysterically, I finally secured Milly inside the house. I returned to find the squirrel with no visible injuries except that his back legs no longer seemed to work. I intended to scoop up the poor creature into my flat shovel and put him out of immediate harm's way, on the other side of our fence. As I picked up his rear end with the shovel, however, I discovered that the squirrel could walk on his front legs as long as I supported the weight of his hind parts on the shovel.

Great, I thought, a paraplegic squirrel!

I momentarily wondered if he could be fitted with a little wagon for his rear end like I have seen pictured for handicapped dogs. Meanwhile, with Rocky, as I decided to call him, providing the locomotion and me providing the elevation, I followed him to the trunk of a nearby tree. With his claws, he pulled himself up into a large hole near the tree's base. I peeked inside to see that his back legs were dangling out, stationary. I could also see that there would be no removing him easily from his chosen hiding place. I placed several lawn chairs around the tree to protect him from the dogs and put a bowl with some water and birdseed inside. I said a little prayer and left Rocky alone.

All was quiet for the next few days. I headed out for a walk one afternoon when I spotted Milly in the backyard again, barking incessantly and jumping up at the base of another tree. High above my head, I could see a squirrel inching up the tree at an awkward gait. It was Rocky! Then, to my horror, the poor creature began sliding down the tree in an awkward series of slanted positions, like a series of forward- and backslashes on a keyboard. After skidding down the tree several feet, poor Rocky made a desperate arc-shaped lunge and catapulted to the ground. It looked like a shoot-out from a Western where the cowboy is shot, staggers, and falls down with a dramatic thud. Poor Rocky!

I opened the gate and ran into the backyard, shrieking at Milly while the squirrel stared ahead, alive, but in a state of shock. For the second time in two weeks, I shielded him from Milly's wrath, securing her back in the house. I yelled for my husband, Perry, to help deal with the aftermath. I will say that while Perry and I have a fairly equitable relationship when it comes to most things in our marriage, something chivalrous manifests inside him when it comes to dealing with dead or injured animals.

I felt so sorry for Rocky! Even though he and his squirrel friends made a nuisance of themselves by eating the sunflower seeds from my birdfeeder and gnawing on our deck railings, I would have never wanted things to have ended this way. I had tried to help Rocky by getting him to a safe place where he could heal, but he chose to venture back out into the danger of the yard again. I couldn't be mad at Milly, either, since she was just doing what came natural to her breed. She's a hunter, after all, and a damned good one at that. Still, it is painful to watch such primordial instincts unfold in a collision of nature. Survival of the fittest can be a cold, hard dose of reality any way you look at it. It makes me wonder sometimes if God doesn't feel the same way about us, when He sees our own human instincts come out, when we are selfish and cruel and unlovable creatures. Or when he tries to help us, and, like Rocky, we simply do not listen. Human beings tend to think that they know what is best. Do you think there's a chance that God sits back and takes a deep breath, saying, "Oh, give 'em a break. They're just doing what those people do."

I think it's possible. Yes, that's definitely what I think.

CHAPTER 3
HIGHWAY ONE

"I keep a large map of the world hanging above my bed. Everybody wants to own land, but I want to own the oceans."

—Jarod Kintz, This Book is Not FOR SALE

Susan Swicegood Boswell

REDUCTION COOKING

www.girlfromgoatpastureroad.com – January 20, 2014

Even if you're the most amateur of foodies, you are probably familiar with the term "reduction cooking." This culinary technique involves simmering a liquid on the stove until it thickens and its volume is reduced; what does not evaporate becomes more concentrated. The unique combination of the ingredients and experience yields a product that is richer than the sum of its parts.

In life, this process is not unlike "trial by fire." For most women, these middle years can be a time of stress and transition. If my own chemical composition could be examined microscopically, I am certain it would look very different now from how it appeared 20 years ago. I have stood shoulder-to-shoulder with my women friends as we have each come undone in our own ways. A friend who enjoyed nearly 50 years of a solid marriage watched it dissolve inexplicably before her very eyes. Many of us have had health scares. Some have lost homes and incomes. We've lost parents to disease and old age, and lost our children to everything from substance abuse and mental illness to simply growing up. The generation before us is thinning in numbers and we find ourselves being catapulted to the front of the line.

Our sense of loss is not limited to the human beings among us. We've had our pets now for 15 or 20 years; even they are dying in droves. My Australian schnauzer had a stroke last year and surgery this summer at age 18. In people years, he's older than Rip Van Winkle. He can barely find his food bowl anymore. I shake the food around, hoping the noise will attract his attention. When I call his name, he looks in every direction except the one I am calling from. Since he has also lost the ability to alert me when he needs to go outside to use the bathroom, I have begun laying down bath towels in his path, hoping I will fool him into thinking he is actually standing outside in the grass. Washing towels all the time has proven to be a much better option for me than cleaning his previous choice of place to relieve himself: the living room rug. Now my home looks and smells like it did when my son was a baby; the scent of Clorox permeates the air. Baby gates are secured in all the doorways, and medicine droppers fill the kitchen windowsill.

I know I am not alone in my struggles. With so much going on in our lives, my friends and I are surprised to discover that we've also lost ourselves along the way. We were simply too busy to notice. I don't have to tell you this is a scary place, but I do want to assure you that there is no need to be afraid.

This process of "trial by fire" has a secret and often overlooked component. In the midst of giving up so many false forms of security, we find surprising strength in places we didn't even know we had. We have discovered an inner resilience. We still have the ability to learn and excel at new skills and have become better at setting boundaries that help us navigate difficult situations without getting so emotional and personally involved. We have even found that stripped of much that we hold precious, we are still standing, only a little worse for wear. We've found support from all four corners of our lives because during those years we were serving on committees, dropping off food when someone was sick, and babysitting a friend's kid, we were really building relationships that have nothing to do with the business of life, but everything to do with its foundation.

Recently, I lamented to a friend my lack of feeling worthy to enter this new phase of life. I thought by now I'd have it all together. I thought my 401(k) would have another digit. I thought I would have stayed a lifetime member of Weight Watchers. I thought I would have learned to wash the dishes as I go rather than letting them pile up in the sink. I thought I would floss my teeth every single night. Somehow, I thought I would have accomplished so much more by now.

My friend said that maybe we're not supposed to grow up and become like those older and wiser people. Maybe we're not supposed to grow old but should put our intentions on growing young. What if the secret to remaining vital is willing ourselves to stay vulnerable, to stay silly, to continue to love and have faith in the hard parts and to simply not take life so seriously? Maybe in our ideas about growing older, we have it all wrong.

As a result of our struggles, I've seen a new beauty emerge in my friends. Not the same type of beauty we had when we were younger, but more of a reduction cooking type of beauty. An essential and deeper kind of beauty that leaves behind the extraneous and radiates like a tree standing tall and strong in the forest, a weathered rock, the scent of cucumber and freshly grated ginger, a sunrise. It's a glow that comes from within. It has nothing, and everything, to do with the temperature.

BIG LOVE

www.girlfromgoatpastureroad.com – February 17, 2016

Out of the blue, my friend Mr. Edmund used to ask, "Susan, what is this thing called love?" He was 93 years old at the time, which was still very young for him, unlike some folks who are dry and crumbled before age 40. His words were an allusion to an old song made famous by Frank Sinatra and Cole Porter. After a friendship spanning many years, I knew his question was primarily rhetorical and that if I waited long enough, he would answer it himself. I would smile and say nothing, pretending I didn't know the answer. "It's a mystery!" Mr. Edmund would finally exclaim and indeed, even after his passing, it still is.

I have a pretty bouquet of roses on the table from my sweetie and my belly is full of chocolates. I made Perry his favorite cake and showered my kids with Starbucks coupons. Both Valentine's Day and my friend Mr. Edmund have come and gone and still I am left wondering, "What is this thing called love?"

I was recently thinking about my honeymoon. Perry and I traveled to Maine and Cape Cod, two fresh-faced college kids who dared go where not many Southerners had gone before: far north, across the Mason-Dixon Line. After two weeks on the road, we were broke and homesick and stopped for a night's stay at a little motel on the New Jersey Turnpike. The place was a dump, one step above a truck stop. Hell, it may have been a truck stop for all I knew. I remember the woman at the registration desk looked scary with her dyed, frizzy hair, and the cloud of smoke that did *not* surround her like a halo.

Upon entering our room, I shored up the door with a chair. I'm still not sure the proprietor wasn't running a brothel. Among other issues, I recall that our room had a broken window and some plumbing problems. It was getting close to dinnertime and Perry suggested we go to McDonald's. We were newly married and I didn't want to burst his bubble, but we'd eaten at McDonald's with increasing incident due to our decreasing funds. I was sick of it. I simply could not stomach another Big Mac. Now I'm not a person prone to outbursts, or at least I wasn't then, but for reasons unknown to me, I threw myself on top of my husband and began pounding on his chest, screaming, "I am not going to McDonald's. I hate McDonald's!"

I still recall the look of surprise on his face at my clenched fists. We didn't go to McDonald's again for a long, long time.

It's been nearly 32 years since that hot August day, and in that time, my husband and I have weathered our share of ups and downs over things far more important than a hamburger. We've spent time being both the bug and the windshield. Along the way, I've learned that love is not for sissies. Love requires frequent and generous doses of patience. Love reminds me that even when you've known someone for most of your life, there are always new things to learn about them. Most of these things you will find endearing, but some things will drive you crazy over time, as mercilessly as a dripping faucet. I've learned that for love to last, it needs plenty of breathing room. I've learned how laughter can be the saving grace that stops you from killing the person who at times seems put on this earth just to drive you ape-shit.

During those early years of our relationship, love seemed relatively simple. Over the years, however, it becomes weighted down and more complex with a growing family, mortgages, careers, and the accumulated things that hurt us and can be hard to forget, even when they've been forgiven. We traveled a long way from home in those first few years, but we have come further than I would have ever imagined. Love changes. Ours did. If you're lucky, it will trade in the sharp corners of its youth for something more rounded and subtle and less prone to breakage (like something as simple as a piece of charbroiled meat on white bread). Love on the other side never fails to amaze me at its vastness, how it permeates your home and your address book and your outlook on life. How it scatters on the floor like toenail clippings and spreads out your front door and into the neighborhoods and lives off your friends and coworkers. How it's like traveling on a trip where it takes one person to drive and the other to read the road map.

Susan dedicates this piece to the memory of her friend and employer, Edmund William Koury (October 16, 1922 - January 12, 2016).

EMPTY NEST

Greensboro *News & Record*, "Personal Adds: 'Parents Cope When Son Leaves the Nest'" – August 2, 2013

My husband and I are on the cusp of being empty nesters. I'd be lying if I didn't admit that we're giddy with anticipation. We joke about how we'll cope.

Will we recognize our house when we wake to find it in the same condition in the morning as it was when we went to bed? Will we miss the pack of teenage elves that magically descend upon our home between the hours of midnight and 6 a.m., raiding the contents of the refrigerator and strewing the kitchen countertops with half-empty soda cans, Pop-Tarts foils, and Easy Mac wrappers? Will my husband suddenly feel rich when he no longer has to constantly replace his missing bedroom shoes, socks, and razors? How brazen will it feel for me to leave my cell phone charger out in plain sight rather than hiding it in the depths of my lingerie drawer to prevent it from being borrowed? How much time will be saved when I can simply vacuum under my son's bed without first sweeping out a pile of garbage, including scratched CDs, discarded backpacks, a pizza box, and last year's overpriced T-shirts?

As parents, won't we feel smug when he's finally doing his own laundry? Cleaning out his cat's litter box? Will we achieve a sense of satisfaction knowing that he is finding out "what it's really like"? I am fairly certain, however, that if my own parents were still alive, they'd swear that at 51 years old, I still haven't learned that, either.

On the other hand, I'd be lying if I didn't admit to feeling a bit blue. Twenty-one years of watching my boy grow up have passed by in an instant. If letting go is supposed to be a long and gradual process, how did this moment get here so quickly?

This is not to say that I wouldn't have liked to fast-forward through some of those angst-ridden teen years or linger for a few moments over the smell of baby powder or the sight of a toy box filled with plastic dinosaurs, Power Rangers toys, and *Goodnight Moon*.

Like all families, we've had our difficult moments.

Like the time our son says we kidnapped him and forced him on a cross-country road trip through the Midwest, or when, on the same trip, I glanced longingly at the train station outside of our hotel room and fantasized about sending his butt home. Or when he wore black T-shirts and refused to cut his hair for what seemed like an eternity. Or when I embarrassed him in high school by repeatedly shouting goodbyes to him from the car when I dropped him off and he refused to say goodbye to his mom like a proper young man.

Over the years when he has lamented his pitiful living conditions, I've told him that if we had made it too comfortable for him at home, he'd never want to leave and discover his own life. The other night, while packing up the contents of his room, he muttered something about "never coming back." This hurt my feelings at first until I realized that except for a weekend here or there, it's probably true.

Still, his dad and I are excited that he's ready for this next transition toward adulthood. We know he is not being pushed out of the nest prematurely or trying to fly when his wings aren't strong enough. We're so proud of all he has done to get himself to this point and for the person he is becoming. And while I'm sure he'd prefer to remain anonymous, as a proud mom, I can't help but exclaim in a voice loud enough for the world to hear, "Congratulations, Brennen Boswell! I love you. You make your mama proud!"

TAPESTRY

www.girlfromgoatpastureroad.com, "Hanging on by a Thread" – January 9, 2016

The universe weaves a magnificent tapestry. It is multidimensional; no two stitches or colors are the same. The shuttle moves back and forth, strands overlapping and then moving apart. When one thread runs out, another seamlessly begins in its place. Were it not for each and every warp and weft, the tapestry would be flawed, and yet the tapestry is perfect. The tapestry is divine. This is God's work and we sense it, we search for it, we believe in it through faith.

John Lennon once said, "Life is what happens to you while you're busy making other plans." Cocooned by the existence of our solitary lives, we live most of our days in routines of familiar comfort. We get out of bed. We feel stressed about work. We cook dinner. Clean the dishes. Get married. Go to college. Have babies. We think we're fat. Life seems to go on and on. The mere act of living can be so distracting that we forget that life is so precious and fragile until something comes along to shake us from our complacency. It could be a lump. A diagnosis. An accident. Or simply hearing someone say that they are growing weary of this world. Those are the moments that our awareness shifts. We hold on by a thread because it occurs to us that all we have to offer is so very small. A visit. A card. A hug. Maybe a meal.

Such small, insignificant things.

I recently visited an elderly friend. Four months ago, he broke his leg, ruptured a disc, and is now going through rehab. He feels so very tired, just plain worn out. "Susan, I'm ready to cross the river," he says to me with increasing frequency. He laments how he has lost nearly everyone, and it's true. He's lost his parents, his brother and sister, more cousins and friends than he can count. Still, I know this game; we've played it before. "I'm so sorry you feel bad," I say as I pat him gently on a hand that has been bruised by blood thinners. "But it's not your time ... You look too handsome."

Eventually, I get a smile out of him.

For the moment, however, I simply want him to feel better even though he is looking pale sitting in his old recliner with a blanket pulled up to his chin. We talk mostly about what is going on in my life: the dancing lessons I have begun taking with my husband, about the holidays spent with our respective families, about my son and his fiancée, about my pets. My friend swears he wants to come back in his next life as one of my pets. I laugh because he thinks they have it that good.

Later, I reflect on this scene. One minute we are talking about dying, and the next, I'm talking about the fox-trot. It seems so easy in that moment, like life and death are one and the same. There is no fear.

That is the moment I catch a view of the tapestry.

Western culture positions life and death as mortal enemies. We forget that life is not the thread any more than death is the absence of one. Life and death are each one human experience twisted into a single strand. Life and death are, of course, inseparable. We sacrifice our mortality to be woven into the whole.

I know about everlasting life. I know my name is written on God's hand, but as the frail and imperfect human being that I am, I am prone to worrying over life's earthly details. I believe we were made in God's image, but could it be the other way around sometimes? What if, like me, God's eyesight isn't so good anymore? Does he need a magnifying glass or to borrow my readers?

CHAPTER 4
FLAT TIRE

"No matter how I look, the freak inside me leaks out."

—Marisa Coughlan

BALLERINA

www.skirt.com/susan-boswell – March 1, 2009
www.girlfromgoatpastureroad.com – March 9, 2016

As a child, I dreamed of becoming an elegant ballerina, however it was one of those things in life that was not meant to be. For years, I begged my mother to let me take dance lessons like my childhood best friend, Debbie Koontz. My parents refused by saying that the dance studio was located too far from our house on Goat Pasture Road and besides, dance lessons were too expensive. Mother also did not feel that I needed to be a ballerina since she had already discovered my talent. Our family had inherited an old upright piano from my paternal grandmother and I had played it out of sheer boredom for most of my life. While I could easily capture any melody by ear, my form was stuck in the basics of chords and one-finger pecking.

Consequently, instead of dancing, mother signed me up for piano lessons while Debbie Koontz took the dance lessons I wanted for myself. When we spent the night together, Debbie would show me all the steps she had mastered: the shuffle steps of tap, the jazz hands of jazz, and the holy pliés of ballet. I remember coveting Debbie's beautiful recital costumes, full of sparkle and froth, as well as her pale pink ballet slippers. It was like a mark of womanhood when Debbie went through the dancer's rite of passage and finally received her first pair of pointe shoes.

⇌

More than 40 years had passed since my last sleepover at Debbie's house and I'd never forgotten how much I wanted to be a dancer.

Upon learning that Devon, a friend of my son's, was taking adult ballet lessons in nearby Clemmons, I shared with her my childhood story. "Come to class with me," Devon encouraged. I declined. "But Susan, this class is not for people who have danced all their lives. Everyone's a beginner. Besides, there is a mix of ladies in there. In fact, one of them is a mom like you."

My eyes lit up. What a great idea! I could do this. I briefly considered my health. I was not in the best shape. "Ballet for adults" is obviously not without its risks. In addition to the potential damage to my self-esteem, there would also be a risk of real physical injury. Regardless, I had made an oath to myself on the verge of my golden years that I would live large and that I would not cower in the corner of the room, afraid to be a risk-taker. I figured that if I had the chance to mark something off my bucket list, I was going to do it.

On the evening of the class, I was a bit late leaving work. When I got home, I couldn't decide what to wear. "What to wear?" has been the eternal question that has plagued me for every event in my life. When I die, would someone please remember to etch those words onto my tombstone and make this final wardrobe selection for me? I called Devon to ask for advice. She suggested I wear yoga pants and thick socks. I perused the drawer of my casual pants. Hmmm. I wasn't 100% clear on what she meant by "yoga pants." I owned one pair of gray sweatpants that were slightly flared at the bottom, but they didn't seem very danceable. Since it had been a warm day, I thought maybe I should wear something cooler. I didn't have a lot of suitable clothes to choose from. Finally, I found some beige capri-length pants and paired them with a white V-neck tee and my metallic flip-flops.

I also did not own a full-length mirror, but I could tell from the view of my upper half in the little bathroom mirror above my sink that I looked decidedly "un-ballerina-ish." I needed some drama. I needed to look like the girls on *So You Think You Can Dance.* Maybe

I needed to channel Jennifer Beals in *Flashdance*. I remembered an orange and lemon sherbet-colored infinity scarf that was buried in my closet, so I dug around until I found it, and wrapped it around my neck and shoulders. I felt that I looked a bit more like a dancer although, unfortunately, not like a ballerina.

I drove like a mad woman to Devon's house. I'd forgotten my socks, so I called ahead to ask Devon if she'd let me borrow a pair of hers. As she slipped into the car and buckled her seat belt, she gave me the once-over out of the corner of her eye. I could tell I had missed the mark on the wardrobe. Sensing her disappointment, I began explaining the confusion over the pants and the scarf. Devon seemed more concerned that no one would be able to see my knees, which I considered a blessing. That was when I realized that Devon was wearing a black leotard with her yoga pants, and that I had failed to understand the complex layers of a ballerina's wardrobe. Then she confessed that the only clean socks she could find were either toe socks or tube socks. My mind flashed back to the multi-colored toe socks I wore in 1976; every toe was a different color. Thank God she decided to forego the toe socks, but I could tell that the purple and pink-banded tube socks she brought me were not going to match the sherbet hues of my scarf.

We arrived at the dance studio with seconds to spare. I entered, feeling awkward, and began looking for the other mothers. The instructor asked me if I planned to dance and I assured her that I did.

I had not dressed up for nothin'.

I spotted some glittery costumes and accessories in a basket, but Devon discouraged me from inspecting them too closely. Instead, she instructed me to put on my mismatched tube socks. I decided that rolling them down might be more comfortable and make me look less like a deranged football player. Although my knees did not show, if the instructor was quick, she could catch a good four inches of my lower calf.

At Devon's suggestion, I removed the scarf.

"Gosh, there are a lot of mirrors in here," I thought as I gazed around the room. The barre on the wall was mounted so high, I asked Devon incredulously if we would have to put our legs up on it. Honestly, I could have hung upside down on it like it was a monkey bar. My next thought was that before we got started, I needed to find a bathroom. Even though I was a newbie, I knew that incontinence and ballerinas do not make good dance partners.

The instructor suddenly called the class to attention and we made our way to the dance floor. I was concerned because there did not seem to be any other moms in the group. There were five students in the class: Devon, three high-school girls, and me. "Where's the mom?" I whispered to Devon, and she gestured toward one of the girls I thought was in high school. The "mom" was 30, at most. She wore the same wan expression atop her waif-like body as all the other dancers. "Geez, am I the only one here with breasts?" I wondered. I tried not to look at myself, but there were so many mirrors, I couldn't help it. The other girls looked like real ballerinas in their black leotards and pink ballet shoes; I looked ready to go grocery shopping.

The music started. Our instructor, another waif named Mary, explained the correct posture for ballet. From her instructions, I ascertained that my bottom half needed to spread out like a castrated frog while simultaneously relaxing my shoulders. Mary began shouting a series of rapid commands. It was very hard to follow and so I tried to imitate Devon's movements. Mary shouted, "Plié, grand plié, demi-moore plié, and relevé," and combined the moves with a confusing number of various feet positions numbered one through five. Then, while our feet played "Twister," our arms were supposed to do an elaborate series of Vanna White moves. Doing a reenactment of the world's most wacky game shows, I elaborately gestured to the letter board on my left while the crowd screamed "*Wheel! Of! Fortune!*" Then I performed a big reveal to my right, a move garnered from *The Price is Right*: "Here, behind Door Number 3, your brand new car!" And then the third and most humiliating move of all: something from *Let's Make a Deal* that resembled, "I'm gonna cover my head with this tiny umbrella!"

Yes, it was overwhelming, but I tried my best to keep up. I am not a quitter, unfortunately, even when it would be in my best interest to be so. Obviously, I was traumatized and delusional. Somehow I thought I was doing OK until we performed the coup de grâce.

We lined up at the short end of the studio. Mary changed the music to something that sounded like the composer was "hyped up" on too much caffeine. She commanded us to perform a routine whose locomotion would propel us 30-40 feet across the room to the opposite wall. The moves were like *gallop-squat-hop-slide ... gallop-squat-hop-slide*. Mary looked at me sympathetically and suggested I forego the arm movements, which I wasn't trying to do in the first place.

Suddenly, I realized that I was no longer a part of the group, unable to hide among the other girls. This was like a race and I was losing, big time. I lurched behind the others, sans arms, like a headless rooster. Then, in addition to being unable to master the movements, I made two mistakes: I simultaneously caught my reflection in the wall of mirrors, and saw the faintest twinkle of amusement in Mary's eyes.

I finally saw how truly desperate this situation was.

I completed my *gallop-squat-hop-slide* to the other end of the studio, yards behind the other ballerinas. All of a sudden, I was overcome with emotion; I needed to find the restroom. (The former happens to me on very rare occasions while the latter is becoming more frequent.) I tried to hold both feelings in, but something between hysterical laughter and hysterical tears welled up inside my throat while the other end was welling with something else altogether. My eyes reddened and my face contorted unattractively. Mary looked at me as if she was afraid I was having a stroke. For a minute, I actually hoped that I was, and I hoped that Mary felt guilty for smirking at me just before I died.

I was not spared a quick death.

Somehow I made it home and told my husband of my latest fiasco. We've been married a long time and he is no longer surprised at anything I do. Then, out of nowhere, the emotions I had swallowed in the dance studio began to rise again. I grand pliéd into a full-fledged hissy fit with real tears and a very ugly cry. Hubby looked concerned. Bless his heart, he really did.

"Oh my God," he exclaimed. "This sounds exactly like an episode of *I Love Lucy*." Perry has seen every episode of *I Love Lucy* at least 40 times, no lie. I have no idea what he is talking about. "There was an episode where Lucy wanted to be a dancer," Perry continued. "At the audition, she rearranges all her clothes to look like the other dancers by pulling the neckline down over her shoulders and her pants legs up. Then, she tries to copy the moves of the other dancers…" His voice trailed off and we both fell into a wave of hysterics. "Yes, that's it, exactly!" I said. How had I miscast myself in *Flashdance* when I was really Lucille Ball?

In hindsight, I would still love to be a ballerina, but I've decided that I should, literally, move on. Maybe I will try salsa? Or square dancing? Both Lucille Ball and I are simply too loud and colorful to be good ballerinas, even if we could manage to master *gallop-squat-hop-slide* while simultaneously showing the car behind Door Number 3!

I'M ALL OUT OF PLUCK

www.skirt.com/susan-boswell, "The Eyebrows Have It" – July 4, 2010
Greensboro *News & Record*, "Personal Adds: 'Eyebrows? I'm Just Plain Out of Pluck'" – March 1, 2013
www.girlfromgoatpastureroad.com, "I've Lost It" – June 19, 2015

At midlife, it is generally accepted that for a woman to age gracefully, she must become accustomed to losing certain things. Since I am no longer a teenager, loss is something that I have learned to live with. For example, I have said my goodbyes to my waistline. Karma decided to pay me back for making fun of the elastic-waist polyester slacks my mother wore during most of her adult life. Now it is I who have been reduced to wearing mom jeans with a bit of stretch and a high waistline to contain my bulging muffin top.

I have lost my breasts. Well, actually, they are still attached to my chest and I am grateful for that, but they have morphed into a singular mound of indistinguishable flesh that extends around the circumference of my torso, from breast to back, arm pits to stomach. Unfortunately, my bra only accommodates the volume of the breasts, so every day I must choose which portions to shove into the cups and how much to leave hanging out.

I have also lost the ability to wear cute little high-heel shoes. Last year's platforms that were all the rage at the end of summer sales have left me with a nosebleed. I am afraid that if I wear these ridiculously high shoes, I will fall and break a hip. In fact, it also seems that I have lost the ability to run. I entered a 5K a few weeks ago and my poor ankles are still aching and refusing to bend properly when I walk down stairs. In the future, if you see me running, you'd better run, too, because you can be certain something is chasing me.

I have lost my vision, as testified by the growing pile of 1.5, 1.75, 2.0, 2.25, and now 2.5 readers on my nightstand. Even my sister, who is 11 years, six months, and 45 minutes my senior (sorry, sis, for pointing out our age difference), can see better than I can.

Most likely, I have lost my mind, too, but with so many fluctuations in my hormones, I have yet to realize it.

Of all the things I have lost, the most humiliating thing has been my eyebrows. For years now, they have been silently walking off the job even as their deadbeat cousins appear on other parts of my face like uninvited guests. There is a layer of peach fuzz that has surfaced on my chin and sideburns much like my Sheltie's winter undercoat. There are strange, singularly long hairs that sprout from my jaw like Cousin Fester. There's a long, thin, blonde one that morphed out of my forehead until one day I discovered it lying in a sweet two-inch curl. It's a matter of time before hairs start growing out of my ears and nose. It seems like out of sheer loneliness that all these strange little sproutings could initiate a social gathering and begin to congregate in the vicinity of my former brows!

For years, I have used a secret regimen of dark powder and a coat of clear liquid gel to cover up my brows' bare spots. Until recently, I thought I was doing a great job concealing my "condition." However, a few weeks ago, my husband burst my bubble. He had spent the afternoon with a family friend whom we haven't seen in years. Afterward, I inquired innocently, "How'd she look?"

"Oh my," he confessed. "She looks just like her mother." This elicited a naturally sympathetic reaction from me. "But the worst of it," he continued, "is that she has lost her eyebrows!"

"Oh no!" I exclaimed, my mind racing from my friend's predicament to count the number of individual hairs left above my own eyes. I secretly smiled and thought somewhat smugly to myself that at least he hadn't noticed my problem. "Yes, honey," he continued, "hers are even thinner than yours."

AAAARRRRRGHHHHHHHH!

While commiserating with my friend Kimberly, she told me about her mother, Miss Edith. With a beauty regimen eternally trapped in the 1950s, Miss Edith uses a shiny brown Maybelline pencil to draw a thin, exaggerated line on her now hairless brow line. One day, in the midst of "putting on her face," the doorbell rang. Forgetting that she had one eyebrow on and one eyebrow off, she opened the door to greet her guest. Imagine the postman's reaction when a one-eyebrowed ghoul welcomed him wearing a demure smile and a housecoat!

My girlfriends, most of whom are younger than I am and have the brows of Brooke Shields, have given me lots of suggestions. There are products, they say, not unlike Rogaine, that you can paint on your brows to make them grow. I appreciate their vote of confidence in recommending products that have heretofore been used by balding men, but if it hasn't worked for Matt Lauer, it's probably not going to work for me. I've also dismissed having them permanently tattooed. Oh yes, those same girlfriends have been begging me to get a tattoo, but I don't think getting eyebrows is what they have in mind. These girls have playfully suggested getting my son's name tattooed upon my ankle or perhaps a smiley face on my buttock, but when I think about what has happened to my breasts, I am afraid that a tattoo on my hip would end up below my knees in a few short years.

Perhaps the best advice comes from Miss Edith. Simply slow down and avoid opening the door until you have them both safely and securely drawn in place.

$100 HAIR SPRAY

www.skirt.com/susan-boswell – February 28, 2012
Greensboro *News & Record*, "Personal Adds: 'You'll Pay a Pretty Price for Big Hair'" –March 30, 2012
www.girlfromgoatpastureroad.com – June 15, 2015

Recent unanticipated expenditures in the Boswell household, including the purchase of a new car, have caused my husband and me to take a closer look at our monthly budget. We've cut back on eating out and begun buying day-old bread at the discount bread store. I've value-engineered our cable and cell phone packages, including a rather ingenious intervention on my part that involves cutting off my son's data and texting privileges when he somehow exceeds the "unlimited" plan I spend too much money on anyway.

One of the areas I am most reluctant to cut is the one marked "Health and Beauty." A recent review of my monthly expenditures confirms that the natural look I have boasted for so many years is costing me an unnatural amount of cash. Hair color, styling products, and makeup are expensive!

Having grown up in the shadows of Farrah Fawcett, Cyndi Lauper, and *The Breakfast Club,* I have never relinquished my love for big hair. As a Southern woman of a certain age, I have lived for years under the honor code of "the higher the hair, the closer to God." It's an expression nearly every woman in the South lives and breathes with the same fervency that leads us to proclaim Tammy Wynette as the true Queen of Country Music.

Therefore, when I recently ran out of my favorite salon-style hair spray, I was thrilled to find a huge $9.99 can of something called "Big Sexy Hair" at my local T.J. Maxx. With visions of St.

Peter and angelic '80s pop icons dancing in my head, I knew this was the right hair spray for me. While I was at it, I also splurged for the $6.98 "Sexy Light" shampoo, which promised manageability and control without weighing me down, attributes that would surely help my hair, if not my social life.

The next morning as I got dressed for work, my hair was initially light, manageable, and gloriously big! I congratulated myself on my purchases and began to spray "Big Sexy" all over my newly styled 'do. The first spray from the aerosol can sputtered out in a glob. Giving it a good shake, the second attempt came out in a fierce narrow stream. Undaunted, I closed my eyes tightly and began to spray, my arm doing a series of rapid and elaborate figure eights as I tried to dispel the stream into a spray. I opened my eyes to find disaster!

I had been flocked! Dear God, I looked like a Big Lots Christmas tree, my uppermost branches adorned with mounds of fake snow.

I slipped on my reading glasses and squinted at the fine print. "Big Sexy" was not hair spray at all, but some sort of styling mousse. I tried to brush the snow from my hair, but it was useless. My "Big Sexy" hair had taken a definite turn for the worse.

Later in the day, as I was confessing what I had deemed my "disast-hair," my friend Diane (someone who I can always count on for sound advice) suggested I visit Sally Beauty Supply to purchase professional products at a discounted price. After perusing their shelves over my lunch hour, I determined their hair spray such a bargain, that I purchased two cans. The sales clerk at the checkout told me that for an additional $15.00, I could save 10% on all purchases for the next year. Since I use a lot of hair spray, this seemed like a no-brainer.

The next few days did not go so well. The rain and humidity that saturated Greensboro were not my fine hair's best friend. The hair that held such heavenly promise had taken a harrowing turn, if not toward hell, then certainly toward the flatlands. "What happened to you?" asked another friend, noting my sagging locks. Realizing that my newest bargain hair spray offered no resistance to humidity, I conceded my latest purchase had been no bargain at all.

By Sunday, I didn't care what it cost. Tired of looking like an abandoned pound pup, I was desperate and willing to pay anything. I drove 30 minutes to the mall to purchase my original hair spray from the expensive salon. Perusing the shelves, I was suddenly confused. My old trusty brand now came in two varieties, both offering maximum control. I asked the young sales clerk to explain the difference. She peered out at me dramatically from dark, side-swept bangs. "Uh, this one says 'Platinum'," the eye said while the mouth smacked loudly on a wad of gum.

"Yes, I can read that," I said testily, "but is one of these better for humidity?"

"Ummm, I guess I need to familiarize myself with this product," the eye confessed. "I don't really use hair spray."

Obviously.

I rolled my eyes; it was a gesture the clerk failed to notice because she could not see me through her long bangs. Suddenly, I realized that this person couldn't help me. At this point, only God and Farrah Fawcett could help me. "Give me one of each," I said, handing the eye the last few bucks from my $100 bill. "And a bottle of Elmer's Glue, please, while you're at it!"

THE SPIES NEXT DOOR

www.skirt.com/susan-boswell – August 12, 2010

Did you hear the story last week about the arrest of 10 Russian spies who were caught posing as regular Joes and Joannes in suburban homes scattered around the nation? I cannot help but wonder what kind of international secrets could possibly be gleaned by casing our lives in the suburbs with its carpools, church socials, and backyard cookouts. I hate to burst Channel 8's bubble, but this spy thing is already old news in my neck of the woods. Spies infiltrated my neighborhood way before this story ever broke.

I will share my story with you in the event that they are hiding out in your neighborhood, too.

My husband and I have long suspected that our next-door neighbors are secret agents. We cannot remember who they said they were, so we call them "the Mansons" after that homicidal maniac, Charles Manson. Unlike most of the folks in our neighborhood who throw up their hands as they drive by or chat over the fence when it's time to mow the yard, these neighbors always seem to avoid us, going outside in the evenings when we can't see them well enough to provide a good ID. They leave home through the security of their garage, disguised in a typical suburban SUV with tinted windows, I might add. They return in the same mysterious manner, at the same time each evening. They have a daughter (or someone posing as their daughter) who was an infant one year and then old enough to date the next time I saw her.

I think they must have switched her out for an older model.

Not long after the Mansons moved in, I almost caught them in an act of espionage. It was Thanksgiving night and my hubby, Perry, and I decided to get an early start on a holiday decorating project in our dining room. Perry was painting "Spring Apple Green" along the upper corners of our vaulted dining room ceiling. Poor thing, he doesn't do heights very well. Just as he climbed to the top of the 8-foot step ladder, the entire can of paint came crashing down and splattered all over the wood floor and area rug. While my husband cursed and cleaned the floor, I hauled the dining room rug outside to hose it down in the crisp November air. Glancing toward my neighbor's adjacent deck, I had a clear view into their laundry room.

A backlight shone through from their kitchen, illuminating the silhouette of a solitary figure standing beside the window, watching me. At first, I ignored the Peeping Tom and kept rinsing and scrubbing the rug. As I began to get cold, however, I became increasingly annoyed. "Don't just stand there and watch," I grumbled. "Come on over and help me!" The figure continued to stand there staring at me as if he or she didn't know I could plainly see them through the window. After what seemed like hours, Perry came outside to check on my progress. By this point, it was all I could do to stop myself from going to the neighbor's house, knocking on their door, and giving them a piece of my mind. I filled Perry in on the neighbor's antics. He looked across the yard into their laundry room and back at me. "Honey, that's not a person. It's a bottle of laundry detergent," he said. "It's sitting high up on a shelf. See?"

They foiled me that time, but now I'm watching them even more closely for their next slip-up.

The spies are not only within our neighbors' houses; they are out lurking on our streets and in our neighborhoods. One morning around 5 a.m., I was out for an early morning walk when I almost ran right into another neighbor, Mr. Biggs. He was moving stealthily across his yard wearing only his tiny white Skivvies. He pretended to be retrieving the newspaper, but I knew he was really out on some kind of "undercover" mission. Boy, you should have seen his face when I wished him good morning from the dark with that chirpy voice of mine. I am fairly certain that he is a member of the same Russian contingency as those other spies in the news. The faint, guttural sounds of a Russian accent punctuated his voice as he muttered something that sounded like "Bolshevik-Oksana-Sputnik!" before collecting his newspaper and booking it back into his house.

What on earth could these spies possibly hope to learn about the security of our nation through the daily and nightly observations of residents in a typical suburban neighborhood? They might learn that we eat Lean Cuisines for dinner while watching *TMZ*, or that we're addicted to really stupid reality television shows like the *Real Housewives* series and *Keeping Up with the Kardashians*. They might peek through a crack in my window blinds to gather insight into the private nocturnal habits of a typical middle-age couple: me, resplendent in my granny panties, carpal tunnel arm brace, and ear plugs, and Perry, hooked up to his CPAP (breathing) machine resembling nothing less than a Snorlax.

Perhaps they analyze the monotony of our suburbanite schedules, trying to decipher some sort of domestic Morse code:

Tap, tap, tap, tap ... Wake up, work, drive home, eat dinner, sleep, and begin again.

Tap, tap, dash ... Wednesday is the day to take the garbage to the curb.

Tap, dash, tap ... Thursday is grocery day.

Tap, tap, crash! ... Hey, let me in! I'm locked out!

How can those spies even sleep at night for trying to decipher this scintillating information? A more likely story is that they are paid to stay awake while we are sleeping. That is why they prowl the back alleyways of our neighborhoods like stray cats. I imagine that they know who is sleeping with whom and what our children are smoking on the back deck when we're not at home. I'll bet they even know who stole the newspaper out of my driveway last

Sunday morning, and who put their trash in my garbage can when they thought I wouldn't notice. Really, while there is nothing much happening here in suburbia that could be of national interest, it has just occurred to me that there are many valuable secrets to be gleaned of a more domestic nature. Maybe those spies are playing for the wrong team. I wonder how much I would have to pay to get that information?

Quick! What's the area code for Russia?

Author's Note: Immediately after this blog was published, my family and I traveled out of the country to Nova Scotia, Canada. While there, I checked the blog's comment section to discover a surprise entry written by my neighbor "Mrs. Manson." Although we barely knew each other, she left a note that revealed more about my own secrets than hers. She said that she had been following my blog for a while and that she found my stories humorous. Although she knew that I had written about her family, she denied any involvement as secret agents and/or the witness protection program. I, for one, don't believe her.

CHAPTER 5
TRAVELING LIGHT

"I travel light; as light, that is, as a man can travel who will still carry his body around because of its sentimental value."

—Christopher Fry, *The Lady's Not for Burning*

Susan Swicegood Boswell

HAILING A YELLOW TAXI

www.skirt.com/susan-boswell – March 29, 2012
88.5 WFDD, "Real People, Real Stories" – August 6, 2012

As a gift for my 16th birthday, my parents bequeathed me their old 1968 Ford Fairlane 500. My friends immediately dubbed it "The Yellow Banana." It was built like a tank, four doors, of course, and completely uncool, but it got me where I needed to go. One summer afternoon, I was driving The Banana along the country roads of Davidson County to my part-time job in downtown Lexington. On a long and desolate stretch of two-lane road, my car began to choke and spasm. *Ugh-oh.* I had failed to notice the gas gauge registering near empty. As The Banana and I coasted to an undignified stop, I looked around, pondering my predicament. Although I was in central North Carolina, the landscape that unfurled before me appeared more like the endless sea of cornfields and pasturelands that you might see in Nebraska or Kansas. Undeterred, I stepped out of my car and set out in the direction I'd come from.

I had not walked far when from out of nowhere came a yellow taxi.

Now for those of you who live in the city, there is nothing remarkable about a passing taxicab. Let me assure you, however, that in 1978, standing at the edge of a cornfield in rural North Carolina, it was a strange sight indeed. Although I had never traveled to a big city or ridden in a taxi before, somehow I knew what I was supposed to do. I held up my arm to catch the driver's attention.

Looking back at my situation from the perspective of an adult, I now realize that if you are a cute little 16-year-old girl standing roadside in the middle of nowhere, dressed up in a breezy summer skirt and Candie's, the "hailing" part was completely unnecessary.

The taxi rolled to a stop. I peered into the cab at the dark-skinned man behind the wheel. I explained to him how I was on my way to work and had run out of gas. The kind man drove me a few miles to a service station where I called daddy to bring me a gas can. I thanked the cab driver profusely, but he refused to take any money.

Despite having forgotten much over the course of my lifetime, I can still remember that day like it was yesterday. I remember the feel of my skirt blowing against my bare legs. I see the July heat rising off the pavement and the endless sea of cornfields that blurred into a smudge on the horizon. I can smell the taxicab's musty interior and hear the lilting accent of the mysterious driver as he conversed with a voice at the other end of the radio.

My memory of the yellow taxi reminds me of the many times in my life that have I been the recipient of so much undeserved grace that I feel almost ashamed. And yet for reasons we cannot understand, there are other times in our lives when we go through long periods of equally undeserved hardship and struggle. Every day, I hear about good people who suffer multiple and simultaneous difficulties. Perhaps they have lost their job, are facing bankruptcy or the loss of their home or their family, or are coping with illness or addiction.

It seems so unfair.

It *is* unfair.

The Old Testament story of Job tells of an honorable, exemplary man who faced insurmountable and catastrophic losses. Job lost almost everything: his children, his home, his wealth, and his health. It is a powerful story, yet one I have never particularly liked. It makes me feel so small and incidental, unable to affect even the smallest aspect of my own destiny. How often is it that our lives feel out of control? How often do we feel like specks of dust being blown around at the mercy of a great wind?

Yet I also believe, mainly because I have witnessed this in my own life, that there are times in our lives when we are the beneficiaries of a comprehensively undeserved grace. Times that reveal something about the daily mysteries and miracles among ordinary people with an extraordinary God. Times when for reasons unknown, a Higher Power goes before us spreading the cornfields like He parted the sea, and calls forth a yellow taxi, just when we need a ride.

The Long Way Home

CHURCHLAND BAPTIST

www.skirt.com/susan-boswell – August 30, 2013
www.girlfromgoatpastureroad.com – June 8, 2015

From the polished oak pews of Churchland Baptist Church, I sit slumped into the curve of my mother. With a short pencil I found in the hole on the back of the pew, I scribble cartoon drawings onto the church bulletin. Despite my low vantage point, there is much to inspire me. Sunlight filters through stained glass windows as fragments of light flutter around the sanctuary. Jesus as a baby. Jesus holding a little lamb. Jesus suspended from a wooden cross.

Behind the pulpit, the choir sits atop an elevated platform. When it is time for a hymn, everyone stands at attention while the choir director, Russ Griggs, moves his outstretched arms in rhythm to the music. In matching yellow satin robes, the choir looks like rows of goldfinches perched high atop roadside telephone poles. Russ flaps his wings as if to fly away while the others chirp like obedient nestlings.

Between the hymns, the choir sits there as if they don't know we are looking right at them. In fact, they look bored to death, as if they are not listening to Preacher Martin at all. I know how they feel; I don't like listening to him much, either. Every Sunday, he starts his talk out all nice, like he wants to be your friend. He tells a funny story that he claims happened to him during the previous week, but I, for one, don't believe him. What are the chances that every week, the perfect thing happens that fits right into his sermon? He wipes his brow with his sleeve, and sometimes his face gets as red as a beet. The longer Preacher Martin talks, the more worked up he gets. I am not sure exactly what it is, but I get the feeling we have all done something terribly wrong.

I don't think Preacher Martin likes me very much anyway. When I asked my mama and daddy questions they didn't know the answers to, like what happened to those poor little babies that didn't get saved before they died, or about the starving children in Africa, Mama actually invited him to the house for supper so I could ask him directly. Although Preacher Martin smiled at me when he spoke and told me how glad he was that I was asking these questions, his answers didn't make much sense. His God seemed to have a lot of rules and regulations. Even then, I didn't think it sounded right that God would send you all the way to hell on a technicality.

Above the choir, the baptismal pool looks like a big picture window. Most Sundays, it is hidden behind red velvet curtains, but on special holidays or if someone is getting baptized, the curtains are drawn to reveal a beautiful scene. Imagine this: the river Jordan winds its way serpentine-like into a distant horizon filled with mountains and palm trees. The light is soft and dappled like it's evening time. I used to think this background was real, but now I know it's just a painting. The front part of the river is edged in thick blades of grass. Mama said that these were bulrushes and that they grew in the shallow waters of the river where Moses' mama hid him in a basket. I have never seen a bulrush but I imagine that if I ever have a baby to hide, that would be as good a place as any to hide it.

In front of the river Jordan, a low glass wall keeps the water (which is real) from spilling out onto the choir's heads. Sometimes I think how funny it would be if someone turned on that water spigot and let water just pour out over the edge of the glass like when you overfill a glass of Pepsi. I bet that would mess up all those ladies' fancy hairdos and wake up that old man who is sleeping in the back row.

I used to wonder why they needed to build a fake river up there when we had a real one practically in our own backyard. Then I figured somebody would just complain how all that muddy water in the Yadkin would mess up everyone's good clothes. Besides, the current would probably drown them before anybody got saved.

I'll tell you a secret. One time during a baptism, Preacher Martin stepped into the water and his preacher's robe billowed up. He pushed it back down with his hands but I could see that underneath, he had on plain clothes just like everybody else.

Ahead of me sits Patty Wafford. She has always been at least a head taller than me, even in preschool. Patty is a goody two shoes and I don't like how she sits up front with the preacher's daughter Darlene. It nearly burns me up, both of them sitting there like they are listening to every word Preacher Martin says while they share chewing gum. Patty is awfully smart but everybody knows she is a crybaby. One time, our Sunday School class had a contest to see how many different names we could find in the Bible for Jesus. I worked really hard to come up with a dozen or so names, even the hard ones like "Prince of Peace" and "Emmanuel." Let me tell you, Patty's list included more than 100 names. I know she cheated. On the back of my church bulletin, I draw a pair of horns on top of Patty's head.

As the choir sings, I swing my black patent leathers in midair to the gentle tempo of the music.

*"Blest be the tie that binds
our hearts in Christian love."*

I look at Patty Wafford and think how I'd like to tie her to a tree. I guess everyone is tied to something.

ETIQUETTE OF DYING

www.girlfromgoatpastureroad.com – July 2, 2015

What can we really say or do for someone who is dying? How do we navigate the vast chasm that separates life and death?

I have struggled with these questions over the last few weeks as my Aunt Betty Jo's health has deteriorated. Aunt BJ is actually my first cousin who, due to a skewing of generations, I grew up believing was my aunt. Over the years, especially since our own mother's death, Aunt BJ has become like another sister, a best friend, and a mother for my sister Janie and me. It is better said that Aunt Betty Jo is the source of such stability and fierce family love that the thought of losing her causes us to feel adrift at sea without an anchor. She is our Steel Magnolia. Elegant. Beautiful.

Independent. Strong as hell.

I visit my Aunt BJ in the skilled nursing facility that has been her home for the past several months. I have applied a fresh coat of lipstick in an effort to look more cheerful and not so haggard. I have brought her a Fourth of July flower arrangement. The moment I step into Aunt BJ's room, I immediately break down. Between sobs, I offer my excuses. I say that I am angry. That her being sick sucks. That I am so very sorry.

We both know that she is dying. Probably soon. I wonder if I should speak of it and if so, what should I say? I am totally unprepared, at a loss for the right words to say. It occurs to me that there must be some rules — an etiquette of dying — but I am rendered speechless. The one person I know who is the expert on all matters of etiquette is the same one lying in this bed.

Instinctively, I grasp my aunt's hand in mine; it is cool to the touch. I stroke her forehead. I smooth her soft blonde hair like she's my most favorite and beautiful doll, and it is true. Then I share with her my heart.

"There are so many more things I wanted us to do together, Aunt Betty Jo," I tell her. "And so much more that I need you to teach me." I recall how we talked about attending the Spoleto Festival in Charleston, South Carolina, and sharing a weekend in New York City. Indeed, there were so many things I needed my aunt to tell me, stories about our family's history and the missing pieces of my life. I had hoped she knew the answers to the questions that would somehow help knit me into a whole person, into an adult.

Somehow we had run out of time.

I am ashamed. My words seem like drivel, such selfish and silly things for me to wish for during my aunt's suffering. Then I feel her strength flow into me as her words find my lips. "But we will be together again," I say. She nods her head in affirmation. There is a faint setting of her mouth; I am unsure if it is a smile or an expression of determination.

I tell her how all the ladies in our family — my sister, our cousins Patty and Elizabeth, her daughter-in-law, Julia — how all of us will keep the family strong by following her example. Over the years, Aunt BJ did the hard work by building a path that we could follow. "You have taught us so well," I say. "Aunt BJ, you will be with us every step of the way."

I am filled with awe and thanks for the life of this amazing woman.

She reaches into the air, her hands for mine, fragile and translucent as a bird's wings. I look at those hands and admire her beautiful nails. They are her real nails, and even on this day and in her failing health, they are filed and tapered, polished a pale shade of mauve. I notice my own ragged nails. "I'll remember to push the skin back from my cuticles," I say, one of the many practical things my aunt has taught me.

I put some lotion on her hands and rub the excess into my own. There is something about this simple, shared act that feels sacred, and I realize in that moment that love has no need for words. Love speaks for itself. It shows up, a spark of light that is the brightest thing in the room. I know with the kind of certainty I've rarely known about anything, that it cannot be extinguished.

⇌

Aunt BJ's memorial service is a "Celebration of Life," fitting for someone who always knew how to throw a great party. She was as famous for her beef tenderloin as she was for recruiting sufficient "help" from friends and family so that she could be the relaxed and gracious hostess. I will never forget the surprise birthday bash she organized for me on my 50th birthday at her home in Clemmons, with its lovely brick patio and wooden pergola and a dining table that was somehow large enough to seat everyone. I also remember the dinner party she hosted one year when my cousin Adrienne was a little girl. Adrienne peered across the serving table, horrified to discover a whole fish, its eyes staring back at her, draped elegantly across a silver platter and garnished with a radish. I will always remember how Aunt BJ loved music and dancing, her special recipe for sangria, and how she made me feel smarter and more beautiful just by simply being around her. Aunt BJ's *joie de vivre* was infectious, even as she entered her 80s looking as lovely as ever with her signature blonde chignon that never went out of style.

Per my aunt's direction, a short memorial service was held in the sanctuary of Churchland Baptist Church, with a celebration to follow in the fellowship hall. Aunt BJ planned a feast, a catered meal from Stamey's Barbecue with all the fixings and, of course, sweet tea. Friends and cousins helped by bringing a spread of fabulous desserts. We decorated a table with photos and news clippings from my aunt's life and those of her children and grandchildren. Hundreds of people joined us in seeing her off on her journey. Our families' good friend, George Washington Smith, brought his band and played beach and soul music. In those moments surrounded by family and friends, Aunt BJ's spirit was so present that it was difficult to be sad.

Our family has lost so many of its members over the past few years. When we encounter each other, often at a funeral, we lament our shrinking numbers. How many times have we paused to say, "We've got to stop meeting like this"? Now everyone fidgets nervously, wondering who is next. None of us is ready to die.

What is amazing is that even after so much suffering and loss in my family, there is still such a fierce and unmistakable call to life. During one of George's soulful songs, my cousin Patty began tapping her feet to the music. When it comes to losing family members, Patty has lost more than anyone. Within the last two years, she lost both parents and her only brother. Patty loves to dance and knows all of the line dances. We stood there in the fellowship hall of Churchland Baptist Church holding each other's hands, swaying to the music before impulsively joining George at the mike and becoming his "doo-wops."

Later, I was aghast that we had actually danced at Aunt BJ's funeral. At a *Baptist church*, no less. What, I wondered, would all the folks from my hometown possibly think about such behavior?

In retrospect, all I can say is that we were overcome by the spirit. At that moment, we were moved to the expression of pure joy and I've no doubt that our colorful Aunt BJ would have loved it. Yes, there is something powerful and primitive in our human condition that drives us toward the life force. Like our ancestors before us, we sing. We beat our drums. We move our bodies in harmony. Destiny comes at us full-on as the hands of time spin faster and faster. "I did that for BJ," my cousin confides later (a bit mischievously, I might add), and I understand what she means. I am, after all, her coconspirator.

I know now that there is no etiquette for the dying. Until the moment our loved ones transition to the next world, they are the same as the living. Treat them with respect. Let them know they are loved and how they make a difference in our lives. Let them know that they are never, ever alone.

I hold the hands of my cousin. Time stops for a moment and I follow her lead. We share a secret smile and for a while, we twirl.

Susan dedicates this piece to the memory of her beloved aunt and cousin, Betty Joann Swicegood Barnes (September 13, 1935 - July 9, 2015). I love you, Aunt BJ, to the moon and back!

SEA OF DREAMS

www.skirt.com/susan-boswell – October 17, 2012

During a recent evening while visiting friends on Oak Island, we noticed a flurry of activity along the remote stretch of beach in front of our house. The wind carried voices back and forth. Flashlights blinked on and off. We wrapped long sweaters over our tank tops and shorts and ventured out, tripping over driftwood and the remnants of the day's sand castles. We gathered near the edge of the dunes and wild sea oats, illuminated by a sliver of crescent moon, to witness 57 baby loggerhead sea turtles emerging from their burrow and beginning their long, difficult journey toward the Atlantic Ocean.

Preservation efforts for sea turtles along the North Carolina coast have resulted in a rise in trained volunteers who monitor their nesting sites. From their nest near the dunes, we could just barely discern an ever-widening path of bermed sand, built by volunteers to help direct the hatchlings to the sea and to prevent them from wandering in the wrong direction. "October is getting late for sea turtles to hatch," one volunteer explained. "We had almost given up hope on this nest." A second volunteer stood ankle-deep in the surf holding a lantern. "Before vacation homes populated this area," she added, "moonlight reflected on the water would have naturally guided the hatchlings toward the sea. Unfortunately, light from other sources can confuse the baby turtles about which way to go when they leave the nest." She stooped over and began to swing the lantern from side to side above the water. "Only about 1 in 10,000 of these baby sea turtles will survive into adulthood."

We counted as 56 tiny turtles emerged from their nest and plodded helter-skelter down the path before disappearing into the dark surf of the Atlantic. The last to emerge was a tiny fellow moving slower than the others. Even after his siblings had disappeared, "Re-re," as he was quickly nicknamed by the group, remained frozen in place near the nest. The volunteer donned latex gloves and scooted him ahead several feet.

Re-re stepped forward a bit then stopped again. He was so still; I wondered if he had given up.

"This poor little guy is completely worn out," our guide said, sadly. She placed Re-re close to the water's edge. We all giggled as Re-re began madly paddling his little legs, the damp sand invigorating him. Re-re seemed to think that he was swimming even though he had never left the shore. Another boost from the Turtle Lady and Re-re slipped into the velvety Atlantic, trailing his siblings. We turned to marvel at the distance all of the little turtles had already traveled in their short lives. The sandy path from the nest to the shore was completely filled with thousands of tiny turtle tracks.

The next morning, I walked with my friend down the street to a local coffee shop where my cell phone could pick up a better signal. I had a voice mail from the previous evening saying that my good friend and neighbor, Al Thomy, had passed away. I was shocked, surprised. I had just visited him in the hospital the day before I came to Oak Island.

I wept on the shoulder of my friend and blubbered incoherently my shock and grief over the passing of Mr. Al and, alternately, the plight of the baby turtles. In the midst of my sorrow, the two somehow seemed related. Coincidentally, around the same time Mr. Al passed away, Re-re had begun his own journey into the unknown.

If you had asked me years ago, Al Thomy would have been one of the last people I thought would ever be my friend. Our friendship, to say the least, was an improbable one. When we moved from Davidson County to Greensboro in 2011, a mutual friend urged me to stop by and introduce myself since Mr. Al was a famous writer and we now lived in the same neighborhood. I recalled seeing his byline in the newspaper over the years, a slight, bespectacled, middle-aged man. By the time I met him, he had technically retired but had never stopped writing or lost his passion for a good story.

Al, I came to discover, was a sportswriter of national renown. In a journalistic career spanning more than 50 years, he had written for *The Atlanta Constitution* among such greats as Lewis Grizzard and Furman Bisher. The walls of his Latham Park home were lined with photographs, many showing Mr. Al alongside notable sports stars and celebrities that he had interviewed. During his career, he published several books, including a biography of NASCAR driver Bill Elliott. He even served as a pallbearer for Ty Cobb.

While there are very few things that interest me less than sports, I found Mr. Al to be a great storyteller with a captivating personality. Al's parents were first-generation immigrants from Lebanon who never found a place in the society of Greensboro. Al retained the hardscrabble determination of his ancestors and loved telling tales, like the time he went back to his homeland to try to recapture a plot of land his family owned that had been taken over by Hezbollah.

During his time in Atlanta, he traveled the country with various sports teams, encountering a circus of personality types from members of the mafia, to bawdy cocktail waitresses and bar owners, to women looking to attach themselves to his bit of celebrity. Like Re-re, Mr. Al had always been something of a loner. He never chose to get married or settle down. Those of us who were his friends simply became his family.

Mr. Al prided himself first and foremost as a journalist, and as a writer myself, I greatly valued his opinion. While Al could be a man of few words when it came to other people's writing, I know that he was proud to see my work published, and he urged me to keep writing. One day, after he had made a point to hear a piece of mine air on our NPR affiliate, WFDD, Mr. Al said, "Susan, you did a good job on that piece. You really made me *feel* something." This was one of the best compliments I have ever received. Because his praise was sparse, I valued it even more.

After returning home from the beach to say my goodbyes to Mr. Al, my thoughts kept returning to that night of the turtles. I remember how we prayed, "Go to the light, little turtle!" I knew Mr. Al had surely gone toward his own light, as well, to be greeted by long-lost family and friends. I recalled how Re-re flapped his legs earnestly while still planted on the ground. That innocent gesture captured so much of the essence of our human condition — our grand plans, our efforts in futility, our self-determination to pursue life on our own terms when we are often called to another. I thought of Mr. Al's struggles throughout his recent illness and what it must have been like for him to have to leave behind a career that was so intertwined with how he saw himself.

As Re-re slipped into that vast ocean, I wondered if he had felt weary or if perhaps he had been afraid. Turtles have a shell for protection, but Mr. Al was all alone. Still, it is in the shedding of our shells and our willingness to be vulnerable that truly gives life to us as human beings. Love, faith, and a connectedness with others allow us to move toward our destiny and to discover our purpose in a future that holds its own mystery.

Susan dedicates this piece to the memory of her friend and neighbor, Mr. Alfred (Al) Marshall Thomy (August 14, 1925 - October 14, 2012). A world-class sports writer, Mr. Al was a truly unforgettable character.

ANGEL BAND

88.5 WFDD, "Real People, Real Stories" – October 21, 2012

When circumstances left my sister and me with no choice but to move our 80-year-old mother into a skilled nursing facility, the transition went better than we'd anticipated. Until then, it had been a contentious situation. Following her diagnosis with early-stage dementia, our mother insisted on living at home, although she became increasingly frightened and paranoid when she imagined that her house was constantly being broken into. Despite our long-distance attempts to help her manage an increasingly chaotic lifestyle with Post-It notes, phone calls, schedules, and organized pill containers, mother failed to remember appointments and take medications as directed. Mail and important paperwork was constantly misplaced and lost. Despite the nutritious meals we prepared for her and left labeled in her freezer, she subsisted on chicken pot pies and chocolate covered cherries. When things were really rough, my sister and I would bring mom into our homes for a few days at a time but invariably, in a new living environment, it only seemed to add to her sense of confusion.

After that, we tried several in-home caregivers, however, mother did not care for any of them. Our mother was, by nature, an extremely independent woman and she refused to acquiesce to a strange woman living in her house, especially when she viewed them as a rival.

Eventually, a broken shoulder, the result of a nasty fall down the basement stairs, led to surgery and several years' stay at an assisted living facility where her health showed some initial improvements. Mother found that she enjoyed the attention and socialization with the staff and the home's frequent visitors. Also, with her medications and her former diet of Little Debbie's and chicken pot pies regulated, her mood swings and paranoia became more stabilized. Eventually, however, she needed more care than the assisted living center could provide. When a hospital stint was followed by the requisite stay in a rehabilitation center, my sister and I knew we had no choice but to make the arrangements for her move into skilled care.

After researching numerous facilities, we found the one that seemed the best fit for our mother. As my sister Janie rolled mom around Alston Brook nursing home in her wheelchair, she gave a running commentary of the reproduction furniture and framed Bob Timberlake prints on the wall. "Now, mother," my sister explained carefully, "you need therapy to get your strength built up. You're going to have to stay for a while in this *re-ha-bil-i-ta-tion* center."

Mother looked around and then looked up at my sister. Even with a diagnosis of dementia she was not demented. "Janie," she snorted indignantly. "*This* is a *nursing home.*"

Initially, the semiprivate room she shared with her roommate seemed small, but it encouraged her to get out and about. She even had a boyfriend for a while, a sweet man named Mr. Roy who had the most beautiful smile and a knobby bald head that reminded me of Tweety Bird. They would pull their wheelchairs alongside each other and sit for hours holding hands. Every day, they seemed to fall in love again, as they caught each other's eye with a soft familiarity without remembering each other's names. After Mr. Roy passed away, mother had a terrible time. Imagine what it would feel like to miss someone that you couldn't remember having known.

Over the next two years as mom's health declined, she spent more and more time confined to the bed in her room. Her roommate, Mary, was a cheerful, middle-age woman who had contracted polio as a child. The physical deformities of her limbs were so severe that the simplest tasks, opening a drink or changing the channel on the television set, were nearly impossible. On bad days, mother's temperament could be horrendous, and she seemed to take it all out on Mary. My sister and I were mortified at our mother's behavior and when we couldn't get her to shush, we pulled the curtain shut between them and mouthed our apologies to her roommate. Mary seemed to understand that mother's mind was sick and not take it personally.

As mother's condition worsened, the bad days began to outnumber the good, yet we were grateful for the kindness shown by the employees and residents at the facility, as well as friends and family members. Nursing homes often get a bad rap, but if you look beyond the surface, you might just find a lot of love, a family perhaps not so different from your own.

One afternoon, I wheeled mom out to the front porch of the facility. I hoped the afternoon sunlight would warm her body and thaw her frozen mind. The porch was decorated with white wicker furniture and huge baskets of ferns and red geraniums. I sat down in a rocking chair beside my former teacher, high school basketball coach and guidance counselor Coach Kent Crim. Coach K became a resident at this facility after he developed early-onset Parkinson's disease in his early 60s. He is one of the youngest residents at the home and is still as mentally sharp as he was during the years he graded term papers and outlined our basketball plays. These days, his big hands tremble except when he hugs you. Then he is strong again. Often when I come to visit my mom and she is tired or asleep, I play checkers with Coach K. As a rule, we play three games. On the first game, he throws it so that I win. The second game is close but by the third round, I have been set up so perfectly that he takes me down with a series of three or four swift jumps before I've barely left my side of the board.

One of the newest residents, Mr. Eugene, is also sitting nearby. A spry gentleman with an impish grin, he tells me of the circumstances that brought him here. After he was widowed, his family became concerned about him living alone. He had fallen a few times and was experiencing heart palpitations. Mr. Eugene says he likes it here but misses his former home. I admire how bravely and graciously he has accepted his new station in life.

Soon, a group of visitors begin to arrive in ramshackle pickup trucks and SUVs. They shout hellos and exchange pleasantries with the residents and guests as they file past, dragging guitars and sound equipment. Everyone is excited because tonight is the night for "Pickin' and Grinnin'."

At ten 'til seven, we make our way toward the dining room. I take turns pushing Coach K and my mother down the hallway in their wheelchairs while Mr. Eugene totters ahead to get a good seat. As we approach the dining hall, a serious, determined man appears in the doorway. With a mouth shaped like a dash and eyes that never seem to rest, Mr. Everhardt always appears to be in a hurry. Today he is wearing one of his signature caps. I get close enough to see that it says Pearl Harbor. "I love your hat, Mr. Everhardt!" I say enthusiastically, and he nods in acknowledgement. As a World War II veteran, Mr. Everhardt has traveled all over the world and has the hats to prove it. Mr. Everhardt is a gentleman and he holds the door open for us to enter.

We take our seats beside Mr. Eugene and the others. Mrs. Simerson rolls her electric wheelchair in beside us. She speaks very slowly and deliberately; her body movements are restricted by a stroke's paralysis. She is like a wise, caged owl.

The musicians assemble on the makeshift stage. It reminds me of The Grand Ole Opry. On this night, Elvis is there (the elder, not the younger) with his signature swagger. His pompadour shows traces of a Grecian Formula comb-through, slathered severely to one side. His voice is raspy from a recent bout with bronchitis. Little Jimmy Dickens struts around the stage like a bantam rooster. Despite his small stature, he is obviously the leader of the group. He sings some mournful old hymns with a recitation or two. Porter

Wagoner makes a big deal of pretending to invite me on stage to sing a duet with him. I think it is because I was the only woman there capable of moving around on her own two legs and hope it is not for any resemblance I might have to his former partner, Dolly Parton.

I politely decline.

Out of the corner of my eye, I see that Mr. Everhardt keeps shooting me looks of disapproval. I can tell he doesn't like me sitting with Mr. Eugene, the newcomer. Mrs. Simerson mouths something to me, but I cannot hear her over Elvis. I reach over and pat her hand. To an outsider, we must look like a sad lot, and yet sitting here, I am filled with so much joy and peace that it wells up inside me. I know God smiles on us, especially in this place. I clap my hands and tap my foot to the music. The others nod their heads and my mom nods off to sleep.

> *I've almost reached my heavenly home,*
> *my spirit loudly sings;*
> *The holy ones, behold they come!*
> *I hear the noise of wings.*
>
> *...*
>
> *Oh, come, angel band,*
> *come, and around me stand;*
> *Oh bear me away on your snow white wings*
> *to my immortal home.*
>
> *-"Angel Band"*

Susan dedicates this piece to the memory of her mother, Mary Louise Young Swicegood (February 11, 1926 - December 25, 2009), and to the kind staff and residents of Alston Brook nursing home in Lexington, North Carolina.

CHAPTER 6
OVER THE RIVER, THROUGH THE WOOD

"At Christmas, all roads lead home."

—Marjorie Holmes

THE CHRISTMAS TREE

www.girlfromgoatpastureroad.com – December 16, 2014
Greensboro *News & Record*, "Personal Adds: 'Christmas Tree Search Turns Frosty'" –December 22, 2014

During a recent drive down U.S. 421 to visit our son, a student at Appalachian State University, I couldn't help but notice the numerous vehicles zipping past us with Christmas trees strapped to their roofs. It was the weekend after Thanksgiving and the Christmas tree growers in the North Carolina mountains of Ashe County had been hard at work for months. This area of the state produces more Christmas trees than any other county in the Eastern United States and has capitalized on providing a cut-your-own Christmas tree experience for folks in search of the perfect Yuletide evergreen. I could just imagine young families traipsing along rippling rows of stately Fraser firs: Little children sitting atop their father's shoulders and afterward, steaming cups of hot cocoa to blast the winter chill.

I'm ashamed to admit this, but I felt jealous at the thought of all that merriment.

Like returning to my pre-pregnancy weight, cutting my own Christmas tree is one of those things in life that I've completely given up on. It's not simply that my husband and I no longer have little children at home to accompany us on such an outing; it's more that we would likely kill each other wandering among those acres of trees armed with an ax or a chain saw.

Don't get me wrong. Perry and I have a good marriage. We trust each other implicitly on most all matters except the selection of a Christmas tree.

My husband has a pragmatic approach. He believes the Christmas tree and all associated paraphernalia should be acquired, erected, and disposed of with as little effort as possible.

He has been known to bring home sensible six-and-a-half footers, trees so slight that they slip through the door and into the room without our rearranging a single piece of furniture. Every few years, he will procure (without my permission) some new-fangled type of artificial tree, from those he terms "very lifelike" to the openly defiant white wire tree that must be decorated in what he describes as a "whimsical" manner.

My trees, on the other hand, are magnificent natural specimens that occupy a generous corner of the room, much like a baby grand piano or a small hippopotamus. In addition to a little topping, mine often require a little bottoming, as well.

This year, our unsuspecting neighbor Michael Lewis generously offered to haul a tree for us in his pickup from the $25 Christmas tree lot up U.S. 220. Since I am married to the Grinch, I thought it would be a more festive occasion if we all rode together. The three of us could hardly wedge our middle-age bodies across the bench seat, and our first attempt to shut the door hit my husband's hip with a dull thud. He glared at me, a foreshadowing, I later realized, of events to come. I rotated myself almost sideways and the door finally closed, however, it was a bit awkward when Mike changed the gears with the stick shift.

Upon our arrival, the Christmas tree lot was bustling with burly young men lugging trees to and fro, and starry-eyed young couples whispering over their selections. "Little do they know," I thought to myself. "Give them a few years."

Chain saws buzzed as the scent of evergreen and wood pulp filled the air. Hubby immediately spotted a tree on the front row. "I like this one," he said flatly, ready to go within the first two minutes of our arrival. I, of course, would never consider buying the first tree I saw. I made a noncommittal "Umm-hmm" and moseyed toward the back of the lot where I imagined the freshest and most beautiful trees would be hidden. "You stand by that tree while I have a look around," I called. Ten minutes later, I returned and in what I intended to be a gesture of goodwill, I conceded, "OK, let's get that tree you picked out."

"Well, it's too late," my husband remarked, his arms crossed and one eyebrow raised. He was perturbed.

"What? I asked you to hold on to it," I said. This was unbelievable. Honestly, all he had to do was stand there and look remotely interested in that particular tree.

"Well, those people got it," he said curtly. "It's too late."

I found another tree.

The next day, I went to get my hair done by my friend Jim Smith at Changes Salon. Hairdressers, of course, are at the top of a woman's list for marriage counseling. Between handing Jim sheets of foil and his subsequent slathering of chemicals onto my mousey locks, I lamented my drama of the previous day. After hearing me out, Jim proceeded to describe the numerous Christmas trees located throughout every room of his house, both live and artificial. He tells me how he and his wife, Starr, carefully choose their live trees together and how Starr approves each and every decorating decision. In his formal living room, he even has a tree decorated with gold, glass, and crystal ornaments. To prove his point, Jim pulls out his cell phone and shows me a picture of a stunning tree, worthy of the White House. Impressive oohs and ahhs follow. "You don't argue?" I ask, unconvinced. "Nope," he says, and sandwiches my hair proficiently between a small sheet of foil.

Jim is nothing if not well-trained.

I try to avoid looking at my reflection in the mirror, but it is difficult when you are decorated with a headful of silver papers. While Eartha Kitt warbles "Santa Baby" in the background, I think of Jim's wife. Some girls just seem to have it all. I'll bet she has a light blue convertible, too.

Susan Swicegood Boswell

THE GIFT OF REAL

www.girlfromgoatpastureroad.com – December 13, 2014
Greensboro *News & Record*, "Personal Adds: 'Christmas Traditions Make Holidays Special'" – December 25, 2013

I was 12 years old when the first of my three nephews was born. Just old enough, I suppose, to command a little respect in my new role as "auntie" but not so much older that I was completely out of touch with their lives and interests. After I married and began to fancy myself as something of an adult, I became disillusioned over the commercialization of the Christmas holiday. Suddenly, the conventional gifts I had been giving my nephews for years — Best Buy and Radio Shack gift certificates, model car sets, and board games — seemed shallow. I announced that there would be no more traditional gift-giving from their Aunt Susie. Instead, we'd share an experience, an activity or an event, creating memories that I hoped would last a lifetime. I thought these boys would be disappointed at their loss of material goods, but instead they were ecstatic.

For nearly 10 years, we came up with something new and different for us to do every year. We had sleepovers, ate pizza, played laser tag, watched movies, and went roller skating. Occasionally, their young cousin Adrienne would go with us, and in the later years, my own son joined us in our activities. One year we attended the Winston-Salem School of the Arts' production of "The Nutcracker" ballet, where the youngest, Michael, had to be repeatedly prodded to stay awake. Also, the boys still tease me about the year we bundled up in mittens and parkas for a winter hike at Rendezvous Mountain only to arrive to find our destination closed. We ate our picnic in the car with the defrost set on high. There's a photo somewhere of the four of us laughing and clinging to the park's entry gate with the "CLOSED" sign prominently displayed.

Not a Christmas goes by that we don't reminisce about those good times.

Traditions change. Like many families, our onetime inbred Southern family has expanded into a cultural hybrid that extends across oceans and to the nether regions above the Mason-Dixon Line. One Christmas, my nephews simultaneously appeared at our family gathering with the three young women who would eventually become their wives. Suddenly, our new "family" expanded from the backwoods rednecks of Davidson County to include Kate, an exuberant young lady from Boston, Massachusetts; Irene, a first-generation Greek-American from Brooklyn, New York; and the youngest, Melissa, an animal lover and future veterinarian technician from just down the road in Tyro, North Carolina. The girls, of course, had their own traditions and brought a new dynamic to the group.

On this memorable of Christmases, most of the womenfolk had gathered in the kitchen preparing the meal when young Melissa suddenly appeared in the kitchen carrying a live baby pig. Let me explain; even for a country family like ours, having a live piglet in the kitchen was highly unusual. Upon catching a whiff (or so it seemed) of the lamb skewers and tzatziki sauce being prepared by my Brooklyn niece, Irene, the piglet let out a squeal.

If you have never heard a piglet who is afraid of being Christmas dinner let out a squeal within the constraints of a tiny kitchen, let me tell you, it's somethin' else. So startled was Irene by the commotion that she nearly severed her finger.

The evening took another turn downhill when Kate's father, Fran (part of the Bostonian contingency who had come to share the holiday with us Southerners), got into a heated disagreement with the Brooklynites over the Red Sox vs. the Yankees. I am not a sports fan and at first I dismissed the sparring as silly talk. As the insults escalated throughout the meal, Fran, who was perhaps caught up in the moment and ignorant of our more genteel Southern ways, let loose the unfortunate "B" word in the direction of Irene. Although my elderly mother was slightly impaired with the early stages of dementia and did not always recognize the faces around her, she maintained enough composure to realize this action was highly inappropriate. Mother rose to the occasion by drawing all of her features into a stern frown, shaking a Parkinson's-ridden finger at Fran, and telling him to stick it up his …

Well, you get the picture.

Sometimes, it's the years where everything seems to go wrong that are the most memorable. These events seem to sear onto your brain with the permanence and painful sting of a cattle brand. (Side note: Fran comes from such an extremely fervent Irish Catholic family that his parents named their children after the Kennedy clan. There was Robert, John, Joe, and Rosemary. When the baby of the family came along, they were out of Kennedy names, so they decided on "Fran" instead.)

Today, our Christmas traditions continue to evolve. After my nephews grew up and went away to college, it became impractical for us to get together for our Christmas outings. Instead, I began a new tradition of baking the boys huge bags of my homemade chocolate chip cookies. Perhaps they say this just to make me feel good, but of all the gifts they receive, my cookies seem to be a favorite. During the first Christmas following their weddings, I made the mistake of omitting the wives from this tradition, giving the girls what I thought were perfectly respectable gift baskets from Bath & Body Works. Would you believe that those girls threatened me? They surely did. They tossed that body spray aside and grabbed those bags of cookies from the hands of their startled husbands. Now my nieces get their own bags of cookies, exactly the same size as my nephews. I count the number of cookies, just to be sure.

The Long Way Home

While it can be difficult keeping the Christmas spirit alive during the hustle and bustle of the holidays, I try to remember that the best things are the simplest. I bake batches of cookies and share them with neighbors and friends. I treasure the sounds of Christmas: the ringing of bells, change clanging into a Salvation Army pot, the singing of Christmas carols. I love the hugs and greetings of "Merry Christmas" that are exchanged among everyone, from friends to strangers. I especially love the quiet that settles upon my household like snow in the days of late December when there's nothing left to do but watch a movie and take a nap. If you have a family like mine, you will understand how that's really something to cherish.

Susan Swicegood Boswell

SHINE ON

Greensboro *News & Record*, "Personal Adds: 'During Holidays, Let Your Light Shine'" – December 14, 2014
www.girlfromgoatpastureroad.com – December 15, 2014

We live in one of those neighborhoods where almost everyone decorates their homes for Christmas. From late November to January, several blocks of Hill Street in Greensboro put on a resplendent show of Christmas festivity. Cars inch down the road, their passengers gawking at the unique and colorful displays.

Last year, I wrapped the big cherry tree in my front yard with several thousand twinkling white lights. Large old-fashioned bulbs spilled red light over the azaleas and wrought-iron railing while oversize Christmas balls seemed to float midair, suspended on fishing line above the canopy over my arched entryway.

The house across the street rivals the Griswolds'. With the help of a professional decorator and a newly added electrical circuit, endless strands of Christmas lights transform their brick bungalow into an enchanting English cottage. The sloped roof hangs heavy with glistening icicles. Lights strewn on the ground create the illusion of a meandering stream. Dazzling illuminated spheres made from chicken wire are suspended from tree branches like rainbow-colored fruit.

Another neighbor's home resembles something out of Whoville. Trees are wrapped and their branches are punctuated with illuminated exclamation marks of color. Columns are striped like crisp red-and-white peppermint sticks, which melt into pink as their tops spread like outstretched fingers over the front porch.

Two houses down, some 50 feet above the ground, a huge star is cradled between the limbs of an old oak tree. I recently learned that the star commemorates a family's tragic loss of their teenage son several years ago. At random times throughout the year, the star is exchanged for a giant red heart. Although I never knew the boy for whom this star burns, my heart holds a special tenderness for his parents. These lights serve as a reminder to me of the fragility of our human lives and the ultimate triumph of a family's love.

I recently talked with a nurse in the oncology unit of Moses Cone Hospital. When I told her where I lived, she commented that many of her patients like to drive down our street at Christmas following their chemo and radiation treatments. I imagine the sight of the brightly lit decorations lifts their spirits and for a moment, helps them to forget the seriousness of their condition.

On winter evenings, I walk my dogs through the neighborhood, pausing to admire decorations that are as colorful and diverse as the personalities who live in each home. I am proud and thankful for the time and effort put forth by my neighbors in a gift that so many of us can enjoy.

From the ancient winter solstice festivals to our modern-day Christmas, celebrations of light have been observed for centuries by nearly every culture around the world. While many of us are familiar with Hanukkah and Ramadan festivals in the U.S., less familiar is the Japanese Obon festival. I've seen spectacular photographs of hundreds of floating lantern "boats" as they were released into bodies of water where they float downstream. It is believed that the lanterns transport their loved ones' spirits to the spirit world.

As human beings, we are made from the same energy as the heavenly bodies and the Creator Himself. Are we not also meant to shine? Through acts of service and kindness, we are like candles whose flames touch end-to-end. These actions allow us to share and amplify the glow of our individual lights without diminishing our own light. We claim power over the darkness and cast warmth into an otherwise cold and lonely world. We shine to let others know that they are not alone. We shine to bring comfort and to ease one another's suffering. We shine in honor of the sacrifice that was paid to give spiritual meaning to our physical lives on earth. By letting our collective lights shine, we manifest the glory of the divine spirit that is present in all living things.

From Hill Street to your street, may you each have a brilliant Christmas and a dazzling New Year!

The Long Way Home

THE PIANO BENCH

www.girlfromgoatpastureroad.com – December 15, 2014
Greensboro *News & Record*, "Personal Adds: 'A Loving Spirit Lingers at the Piano Bench'" – December 20, 2015

I grew up in the country just down the road from my Grandma Young's house. Before I was born, my grandmother carved off a small plot of land from her 100-acre farm and gifted it to my mama and daddy, just as she did for all three of her daughters. After losing her husband to lung cancer near the end of the Great Depression, grandma's only son, my Uncle Frank, moved his new wife, Johnnie, from the city into his mama's farmhouse. There they worked and lived out the rest of their lives together among our lively and eccentric extended family of aunts, uncles, and cousins.

Ironically, our Grandma Young never seemed very young. For the nearly 20 years that I knew her, she seemed ancient. She never learned to drive a car and walked nearly everywhere she went, always carrying a black pocketbook over the crook of her arm. She wore drab, shapeless cotton dresses, thick stockings rolled down to her ankles, and lace-up black leather shoes. In the summertime or if she were working in the fields, she donned a calico sunbonnet (just as she had done since she was a girl), which covered her head and her long, narrow face. She had lost an eye to cancer and although she wore a glass prosthetic, it never seemed to completely synchronize with the real one. In my memories, I never see my grandma in color. She exists, rather, like a painting in tones of grey, a hollowed out *Whistler's Mother*, staring out at the fields with that singular eye, clouded and unfocused.

Uncle Frank and Aunt Johnnie raised their own family, my cousins Bobby and Patty Young, in my grandma's house. Aunt

Johnnie was beloved by everyone who knew her and was known throughout our family as a saintly and gentle soul with a seemingly endless supply of patience. Patience was a virtue in my mother's family because it was something most all the Youngs lacked, her husband in particular.

Aunt Johnnie also possessed a mysterious and fantastic gift that set her apart from the other women of the family. Aunt Johnnie was a healer who had the ability to talk the heat out of a burn and the itch out of poison ivy. When anyone in the family was afflicted with these conditions, Aunt Johnnie would take them into a quiet room, gently stroke the area with her hands and whisper unintelligible words until whatever was wrong no longer hurt. "How does she do that?" we always wondered, but she never revealed her secret.

Grandma Young, like most of the women in my family, eventually developed dementia. My aunt and uncle had to move her into a nursing home for fear she would wander off or drown herself in the river. Until then, our families had a tradition of getting together at her house for Christmas. After she became sick, and for many years after her death, our families continued to gather at each other's houses after supper on Christmas Eve. Sometimes we'd congregate in the basement of mom and dad's brick ranch and sometimes it was down the road in the small, cramped living room that would always be considered my grandma's house. It seems like we rotated houses depending on which family finished eating supper first. Because my mama burned everything from cakes to iced tea, I preferred eating supper early and going to grandma's, where my Aunt Johnnie was the hands-down winner in the family dessert competition. She made all sorts of delicious cakes and pies, including her famous homemade persimmon pudding and fresh coconut cake.

Aunt Johnnie could also play anything on the piano. She sometimes filled in for the pianist at the 11:00 a.m. church service at

Churchland Baptist. Since there was a piano at grandma's house and an old upright one in our basement, not a Christmas Eve passed without my aunt treating us to a medley of carols. One of my favorite childhood memories is of me sitting on the piano bench beside Aunt Johnnie singing "Deck the Halls" and "Joy to the World."

If you were to make a list and tell Santa all the characteristics that were needed to make the perfect aunt, they would have manifested themselves right there in that single stout and faithful woman. Aunt Johnnie was kind, patient, humble, and generous of spirit. She was sweet and soft enough that I could nestle close beside her on the end of the piano bench without falling off. She never seemed in a hurry to go talk with the other adults or to even fix herself a piece of pie. My aunt possessed the ability to heal and she had the ability to recognize — a sense, it seemed — those of us who felt alone and needed, at times, an extra dose of love.

I remember how Aunt Johnnie swayed back and forth to the tempo of the music. Her fingers moved stealthily and nimbly over the piano keys, her eyes focused on the pages of some old hymnal as her feet pumped away at the pedals. My favorite pedal, even after I learned to play the piano myself, was the one on the right, the damper pedal. It makes the piano sound both loud and soft at the same time, allowing each note to remain suspended in the air a few seconds longer before melding with the others and falling silent. How many times have I wished that life itself had a damper pedal, that there was some way of holding on to the magic just a little longer?

I always remember Aunt Johnnie fondly during the holiday season, but it is with a special tenderness this year. She passed away in February after a stroke and long illness, and a mere five weeks after losing her grown son, my cousin Bobby, to cancer. I hold her and the family she loved so dearly in my thoughts and prayers on this first difficult Christmas that she is gone.

Aunt Johnnie passed away without teaching her "gift" of healing to anyone. All we ever knew was that it was a tradition that had been passed down in her family for generations, and that there were specific rules about when and to whom she could teach it. Not long before her passing, I visited her in the nursing home where she had resided since Uncle Frank died, and asked her about the source of her mysterious abilities. By then, she was too old and sick to try to pass on her special abilities to anyone. It was difficult for her to remember and communicate many of the details but she made it very clear that it was no kind of witchcraft; it came from the Bible.

Memory is the closest thing we have to a damper pedal and I continue to feel Aunt Johnnie's gentle, loving spirit throughout my daily life, especially at Christmastime. In the bustle of the holidays, she reminds me not to hurry so. She says not to worry about the shopping and the decorating. I hear her voice in the old carols like "Silent Night" and "Joy to the World."

During those times I sat with Aunt Johnnie on the piano bench, I doubt she felt like she was doing anything special for me. She was just being herself and sharing her love as she had done for me and others her entire life. Despite her numerus gifts and abilities, her single greatest gift to me was just being present. In Aunt Johnnie's making enough room for me on that bench, I was able to feel truly special.

Susan dedicates this piece to the memory of her beloved aunt, Johnnie Mae Wallace Young (January 31, 1933 - February 20, 2015).

MIA

www.girlfromgoatpastureroad.com – December 20, 2015

I've whispered Merry Christmas to you in my prayers and asked God to bless you and keep you safe wherever you may be. You often appear to me in my dreams, the Ghost of Christmas Past. The memories of so many years gone by still make me smile. But just like the character in the Dickens tale, I awake to discover that the "you" of the past and the "you" of the present are no longer the same. Does the person I knew and loved for all those years still exist? I feel that you've lost your way right now and the thought of that makes me very sad.

I found a photo of us the other day. You were just 15 years old, sitting on the living room sofa, the one that was always reserved for company. You are holding me, your brand new baby sister, and you are grinning from ear-to-ear. If you had hoped for a little brother instead of another sister, no one can tell. I guess God gave you the next best thing in me, a little girl who played as hard as a boy. Did you have any inkling then that the little bundle you were holding would follow you around like a beagle pup in a few years, running around half-naked and barefoot in the summer heat and hanging on to the back of that tractor while you plowed the fields?

We sure had some good times then, didn't we?

I have the letter you sent me shortly after you arrived in Vietnam. It was 1969 and I was 7 years old. I thought it was the best thing ever that my brother had sent me my very own letter from halfway around the world. You wrote it on government-supplied stationery and used your best handwriting (which is usually lousy, by the way) so I could read it myself and show it off. The paper is thin and I can read between the lines now, seeing what you didn't say. You were scared and far from home, hanging on to the memories, hoping they'd lead you back one day. You were a good brother to do that, and I want to thank you for remembering me and for reaching out when you were off in the middle of a war.

And then do you remember that time when Perry and I had a fight after our dog died? We woke up on a cold winter morning — just like today — to find poor old Petey dead. Perry wanted to have the dog cremated, but I was upset, telling him people in my family didn't do that, we bury our dead. I was mad as a hornet and I wrapped the dog in a towel and took him with me down to your house. You were going to help me bury him until Perry called later and said he had managed to dig a hole in the frozen earth. We buried old Petey wrapped in that same towel in that cold, hard ground.

These memories are just a few of the ones I hold, prized possessions that validate the light and the good in you. It nearly ripped my heart out to have to draw that line in the sand with you and say "enough." As the little sister, it always seemed natural to let you call the shots, but I can't go along with that anymore. We both have our own conscience to answer to, and our choices are our choices.

Still, I've lived long enough and lost enough to know that life will find a way of going on in that way it does, rolling over those rough patches in life, smoothing them out with time if you give them light and air and don't let wounds fester. There is so much joy to be had during this season of love and family, and I will not allow my sadness to overcome my joy. I'll keep all the traditions. I will treasure time spent with your children and your grandchildren and will wish that the "old" you could be there to share in that joy. My heart will jump when I see their eyes sparkle at the gifts beneath the tree and I'll remember how you teased me for being that way, too, since I was the baby in the family.

Christmas is a blessed reminder of how we'll all be reunited again one day, when there's nothing left to forgive about each other. I wish you hadn't burned so many bridges, but you'd probably say the same about me. Still, I wonder how it is that you came back from the war, but more than 50 years later you are MIA.

This piece is dedicated to the many family members who experience separation from their loved ones during the holidays. While physical separation is difficult to endure, equally difficult is the invisible heartbreak of our emotional separations. For many families, the effects of drug and alcohol abuse, PTSD, and various forms of mental illness cause undue strain on our relationships with our loved ones. Often, a part of the healing process is learning that there is little we can do to "help" family members who are plagued by these afflictions, especially when they refuse to seek/cooperate with treatment. The suffering experienced by these families can be especially heart-wrenching during the holiday season, a time that is all about connection.

CHAPTER 7
U-TURN

"God is at home; it's we who have gone out for a walk."

—*Meister Eckhart*

TOUDIE'S HOUSE

www.skirt.com/susan-boswell – March 5, 2012
88.5 WFDD, "Real People, Real Stories" – March 12, 2012

The sign read, "For Sale by Owner."

"I don't like it," I said immediately. "I hate white siding."

The 100-year-old house was perched on the crest of a hill like a little old lady waiting to catch a ride. She wore a conservative dress, dark shutters buttoned high to the neck. A lace collar of wrought iron edged the front porch from end to end. The six-panel front door was painted such a specific shade of glossy red, I knew it had been color-matched from Talbots. Towering above a yard that was no bigger than a postage stamp was a large magnolia tree; bags of its dried, leathery leaves were stacked nearby like a row of sandbags.

This was the first clue as to the amount of maintenance this home would require.

The door opened and a woman introduced herself as Susie Palmer. She welcomed us inside and explained that her mother, Toudie, had passed away and had been the former owner of the house. Susie began showing us through each room. The living room was small and formal, its symmetry broken only by a large crack that extended floor-to-ceiling on one side of the fireplace. The dining room, on the other hand, was huge and furnished with elaborate pieces befitting its 1920s era: a 10-foot mahogany dining table, a Victorian sideboard, and an assortment of side tables. Closets and bathrooms were tiny.

I shook my head. I looked at the house and then at my husband. "The house seems so ... well, *old*," I said. I had to admit, however, that except for those few cracks in the plaster, the interior was in great condition compared to the other houses we had seen. Recently refurbished, its walls were a freshly painted neutral and its floors a beautiful dark oak.

We walked into the kitchen and peered through a set of French doors into a view of a backyard garden, the land terraced gently, its contents bound by a low brick retaining wall and white picket fence. White roses and yellow jessamine clung to the arbor over the brick patio. The landscape was like an overgrown bouquet of all the old-fashioned plants my mother had taught me to love: gardenias and camellias, boxwoods, and Lenten roses, irises, hydrangeas, and four o'clocks.

"Wow. These plants would have never grown in that poor topsoil of our house in the suburbs," I thought.

"Just look at this," uttered my husband, spellbound. "You always wanted a garden."

"Honey, I'm moving to the city to simplify my life, not to become a gardener," I said plainly. A trail of ivy crept along the fence and up a telephone pole. I was still not convinced about the house. "I want to sit on the patio and drink wine, not work in a garden. If you want this house, *you* be the gardener."

We bought the house. My husband learned how to garden. Well, sort of.

Perry worked diligently to get the garden in shape, although he didn't always know what he was doing. The first year, he butchered the boxwood hedge into a woody mess and pruned the climbing rose so severely that it died. He didn't know the difference between a perennial and an annual, so in the fall, he pulled them all up by the roots and threw them into the recycling bin. He cursed the magnolia tree and the leaves piled high in the side yard waiting to be raked and bagged.

I sat on the patio, sipping my wine, and held my tongue.

From the beginning, unusual things happened around our new home. We began to notice that each time it rained, we would discover new treasures peeking out from beneath the mulch. Statuary, garden ornaments, rain gauges, stepping stones. Items that must have been there before but which we had simply never noticed.

We began to joke that Toudie was leaving us "gifts."

After moving into the house in June, we attended a neighborhood block party on the Fourth of July. When I introduced myself to a neighbor who had lived on our street for many years, she looked at me, perplexed. "That's so weird," she said, shaking her head in disbelief. "Did you know that you are the fifth Susan to live in that house?" I had not known that.

"No, but I did know that the lady who lived there for many years was named Toudie," I offered. "I guess her real name was Susan. My nickname is Tootie, as well, or at least it was when I was little. I spelled my name differently."

Since moving into Toudie's house, one of our favorite things to do is to walk through the lovely old parks and greenways surrounding our neighborhood. We've discovered deer and cranes along Buffalo Creek, nature nestled among city life right across from Moses Cone Hospital. This past December, my husband bundled up for a walk. He returned shortly after, looking pale. "What's wrong?" I asked, concerned. "You're not going to believe this," he began. "I went to Green Hill Cemetery and walked right up to Toudie's grave."

We hadn't even known she was buried there. "She just wanted to wish you Merry Christmas," I offered.

Eventually, our moving boxes were all unpacked and the decorating completed and I resumed writing, publishing a few pieces here and there. Since I did not find the downstairs layout of the house to be conducive to the privacy needed for my writing, I began making plans to clean out the little attic room for my writing retreat. One afternoon, I ran into Susie Palmer in the park. We stopped to chat and she happened to comment on one of my articles that she had read in the Greensboro *News & Record*.

"Wow! I didn't know you were a writer," she exclaimed. "Did you know Toudie was a writer, too? She taught writing at the college. She always said she was going to go upstairs in the attic and write a book."

Yes, another surprise from Toudie!

Over the years, we've simply grown accustomed to living with a certain presence around the house. While painting our newly installed set of French doors in the dining room, my husband noticed a lingering scent of gardenia, although none was in bloom that time of year. One morning we awoke to find accessories and furniture rearranged in the hallway. My son swears he hears noises in the attic and gets the heebie-jeebies at night when he walks into the kitchen.

Me? I keep finding excuses not to clean out the attic. It's not that I'm afraid of Toudie's spirit lingering around my house, nor do I think she would mind me taking over the attic as my own. On the contrary, I believe she's been very hospitable. It's more that I know that Toudie is going to make certain I finish what she started. She's determined like that, you know.

HITTING THE MARK

www.skirt.com/susan-boswell – June 12, 2015

A few summers ago, my sister and I ventured to the eastern part of the state where our brother had taken up residence in an old and crumbling Southern mansion in an equally old and crumbling Southern town. Our brother Johnny Lee seemed oblivious to the home's abject condition and in fact, the entire house seemed held together by decay. Layers of paint shed the walls like tears. From the windows, cobwebs hung in place of draperies. So much plaster and lath were missing from the home's interior walls that we could walk right through them instead of using a door. I marveled as I wandered from room to room, perplexed as to whether the home might have been mid-construction or mid-demolition.

Johnny Lee had recently fallen into bad times, the result of a bitter divorce, financial woes, run-ins with the law, alliances with characters of questionable intentions, the culmination of years of alcohol and substance abuse, latent PTSD, and what appeared to be some form of mental illness that caused a propensity for discharging shotguns within his home's rapidly diminishing number of upright walls.

Of all the places he could have taken up residence, I couldn't help but think how he had landed in this godforsaken place with the same cursory luck one might experience when throwing a dart. If he was aiming for the bull's-eye, he had certainly hit the outer rim. One day, he was driving through this old town, plunked down some of the money from his Home Equity Line, and bought himself a house. A House, in his mind: a fine old house with a capital "H" in a place far enough away where he would know no one, and more importantly, where no one would know him.

Still, my brother loved his ruins with the same affection a king might regard his palace. Like a lord surveying his kingdom, he put his portable hot tub smack dab in the middle of the home's wrap-around front porch. From this vantage point, he could observe the comings and goings of the town's Main Street. Unfortunately, the sheriff asked him a few weeks later to please not sit out there naked with the lights on anymore.

It was in this same grandiose spirit on that hot August afternoon when my sister and I arrived to help him settle in, that he produced an old tarnished candelabra from the cupboard, placing it, with a small amount of fanfare, in the middle of the dining-room table. He beckoned me, his baby sister, to "run to the kitchen" where he had left a bouquet of summer flowers wilting in the heat on the Formica countertop. No artwork adorned the tops of the old quarter-sawn oak wainscoting, nor did a chandelier glisten from the room's plaster-relief ceiling. Instead, tiny dust particles floated heavenward as the sunlight tried to stream in through the windowpanes now covered with a dense layer of weather-resistant plastic.

Johnny Lee had cooked "dinner," as true backwoods Southerners call the noonday meal; "supper" is the name reserved for the meal served in the evening. I could never get over the fact that my brother, my big ole redneck, tractor-driving, hunting and fishing, and cussing-you-flat-out kind of brother had taken to watching cooking shows in his spare time. In recent years, before he had flown the proverbial coop, we'd actually had conversations over the Christmas dinner table about reduction cooking and parboiling and all kinds of things more akin to Chef Gordon Ramsay than a Chevy kind of man. On this day, however, he had brushed most of his newly acquired cooking skills aside, settling on a traditional working-class menu of roast beef, boiled potatoes, canned biscuits, and pinto beans cooked with fatback.

After dinner, Janie and I took to the kitchen for what is still deemed women's work. We cleaned up as our brother stepped out for a smoke. While she washed dishes, I gathered the array of pans and plates strewn across the countertops. Johnny Lee had used a decade's old cast-iron frying pan to brown the roast, and the bottom was thick with grease. "What you want me to do with the grease in the fryin' pan?" I called out to him.

"Oh, just set it down on the floor," he said, his voice drifting like smoke through the screen door. "The dog'll eat it."

My sister, who, I might add, is a bona fide Junior Leaguer (a proud accomplishment if there ever was one in my redneck family), rolled her eyes as I sat the pan down on the dilapidated linoleum. Johnny Lee's big hound dog lumbered into the middle of the kitchen and began lapping up the grease. "Ick," I muttered as I continued transporting dirty pans and dishes across the room. With a lick of his chops, the dog raised his head and began to turn away from the pan. As I reached down to grasp the handle, that dog quickly raised his hind leg and began peeing into the pan.

"Oh! My! Gawd!" I gasped. At that precise moment, a picture formed in my mind that remains there to this day. Behind the dog, whose awkward stance was indicative of someone making a left-hand turn, my sister was frozen like a statue, her mouth and eyes replaced by three perfectly round "O's". All the while, that dog let loose such a long and steady stream of piss that I swear it steamed up like rain on a hot summer street.

"Oh! Oh! That dog… he just peed in that fryin' pan!" I shrieked, jumping up and down in disbelief. "Johnny Lee! Get in here!" (In retrospect, I owe this hissy fit to menopause, which had left me bossy and emboldened in my later years.)

My brother finally stuck his head in the back door to see what all the commotion was about. In one sweep, his eyes took in the dog, the steamy frying pan, and his two hysterical sisters — one in a state of shock, the other one shrieking. For the first time in recent months, he seemed to put two and two together and get four.

Johnny Lee exhaled a snort like an explicative, then disappeared back outside to continue his smoke. "Oh! My! Gawd! That dog just peed in that fryin' pan!" I hollered again. "John-eeeey! Get in here! Take that pan outside right now!" I could hear my brother snickering outside the door.

I looked down at the floor; it was completely dry. Obviously, this was not the first time that my brother's dog had done its business in the frying pan. I couldn't help but think that with the utmost precision, both the dog and my brother had hit the mark.

TREASURES IN THE ATTIC

www.skirt.com/susan-boswell – February 7, 2012
88.5 WFDD, "Real People, Real Stories": "Love Letters in the Attic" – February 13, 2012
www.girlfromgoatpastureroad.com – June 26, 2015

My husband, Perry, is a treasure-hunter. Our home is filled with all sorts of strange and unusual artifacts from his many trips junking. His numerous acquisitions include table lamps and bottle openers made from the hooves of deer (a little creepy), men's hat stretchers and bow tie collections (precursors of upcoming fads, I am sure), and a tiny scissor collection (certain to be used by our aging arthritic hands). Years ago, he brought home a dusty box filled with old letters and photographs that were pilfered from the remote third-floor attic of an old house awaiting demolition in nearby Lexington.

"Another box of old stuff to clutter up my house," I muttered. "Why are you always bringing that stuff home?" Dust particles scattered across the room and onto my clean carpet as he lifted the lid from the box and began rifling through its contents. "I just think it's sad for these things to be left behind with no one to care for them," he began. "It's like losing a piece of your soul."

For years, the box sat all but forgotten on the bookshelf in our living room. Occasionally, we would remember it and pull a letter or photograph from the box. Faces we didn't recognize stared at us across a span of more than 60 years, sepia-colored images with withered edges. The letters were perfectly folded and creased, a ribbon of elegant script drifting across the paper. Eventually, the box became our little detective project and over the next few months and years, I began typing the letters and placing them chronologically into a notebook.

As we sorted the contents of the box, a story began to emerge. It read like a Nicholas Sparks novel with most of the pages missing. Most of the items were love letters dating from the 1920s and '30s. Photos captured a lively, bright-eyed young woman smiling for the camera. On the back of one photo was written, simply, "The Doctor." The terse writing in the corresponding letter hinted of a broken heart. Another photograph, more recent than the others, showed a serious-faced little girl wearing Coke-bottle glasses. There was also a letter in sprawling, childlike script that began, "Dear Daddy, I fell and broke my glasses ..." It was easy to assume that the child in the letter and the photograph was one and the same.

From the letters, we discovered that the bright-eyed young woman was named Lyndal Denny. While she was pursued by many arduous suitors, including the illustrious Doctor, none professed his love more eloquently than the one who signed his letters, simply, "Red." Elmo "Red" Leonard had graduated from college and was working in Lexington in the family mercantile business. Passionate and exuberant, his writing spoke of many things, but mostly of his adoration for Lyndal. Some letters began with "Girl of my Dreams." "How good a sweet kiss from you would be!" declared love-struck Elmo. The poor guy was passionately, hopelessly, and whole-heartedly in love with Lyndal.

Fast-forward to 1992, nearly 10 years after Perry's discovery of the lost letters. We were ecstatic over the expectation of our first child, however, there was one problem. As a public school art teacher, my husband associated every popular name with an unruly middle school student. We finally settled on two uncommon names: "Brennen Scott" for a boy and "Lyndal Claire" for a girl, after the young woman in the letters.

One day, we decided on a whim to try to locate Lyndal's former home. The address was written on the envelopes and we recognized the address to be about an hour away, in the town of Burlington. We were able to locate the correct street but no corresponding house number. A few blocks away, we encountered an elderly gentleman who was mowing his grass; we stopped to ask if he knew of the Denny family. The man said he had lived in the area most of his life and while he was unsure of the whereabouts of Lyndal, he remembered that she had a sister who still lived in town.

We spoke with her sister on the telephone and ascertained the whereabouts of Lyndal. Imagine our surprise at learning that Lyndal Denny was alive and well, living with her daughter less than an hour away, in Durham. We were thrilled when we actually had the opportunity to meet her a few months later and to return the letters to their rightful owner.

Lyndal was already someone who we felt we knew intimately. We had read so many of her thoughts and knew of her adventures, yet we had so many questions. Did she marry Elmo? What had her life been like? Was she happy?

We drove to the retirement community near Duke University where Lyndal and her daughter Harriet lived in a small townhouse. At 89 years old, Lyndal was no longer the same beauty in the photographs, but she was just as vivacious. A blue chiffon scarf was knotted neatly around her neck and echoed the same shade of azure as her merry eyes. Her silver-white hair and clear mind shone with the brilliant patina of old age. She and her daughter welcomed us into their cozy home that overflowed with books and antique furniture. Lyndal graciously accepted the return of her letters as Perry explained how he found them in the attic.

Then Lyndal began to tell her story.

Lyndal was no child of privilege. Her parents and four siblings moved to Burlington from eastern North Carolina in the early 1900s; her father died unexpectedly soon after. Although her mother ran a boarding house and worked as a seamstress, she was unable to provide for her two oldest daughters. It was decided that

Lyndal and her sister would go live in an orphanage. What could have been a horrific experience was made better by the girls having each other. Their mother sewed clothes for them and visited when she could. Lyndal was smart and ambitious, excelling in her classes. When she became older, she worked in the school's administrative offices and eventually earned a scholarship to Chowan College.

While Lyndal was pursued by many young men, she was eventually wooed by "Red," a man with bright auburn hair and a grand sense of humor. She was the love of his life and they were happily married until his passing some 20 years before our meeting. Their only daughter, Harriet, was indeed the little girl in our photos. Harriet eventually became the head reference librarian for Duke Divinity School. Still wearing similarly thick Coke-bottle glasses and a wan smile, Harriet sat quietly beside her mother. She had not changed much in 60 years.

I asked Lyndal about her unusual name and confided that if we had a baby girl, we planned to name our daughter after her. She clapped her hands in delight then inquired whether "Elmo" or "Red" was on our short list of boy names. "No," I confessed, and she chuckled at my reply.

"My mother found the name Lyndal in a book she read before I was born," she said, "but she could never remember the title. Now, Elmo was named after St. Elmo's fire." I tried to reconcile the 1980s brat pack movie and her husband, who had likely been born more than 70 or 80 years before. "Oh, not the movie, of course, but actual St. Elmo's *fire*," she explained. "Have you ever heard of it? It's something like balled lightning that occurs in nature during a storm." Her voice trailed off as her eyes twinkled with memories. "And he *was* a ball of lightning!" she laughed. "Really, it was all very romantic!"

Weeks after we reunited Lyndal with her love letters, I gave birth, not to a little girl, but to a healthy baby boy. Our son,

Brennen Scott, will turn 20 in April. Over the years, we formed a friendship with Harriet and Lyndal, sending them cards on their birthdays and at holidays and occasionally making the Sunday afternoon drive to the beautiful Duke campus where we took them out to eat and shared stories.

Lyndal Denny Leonard passed away four years after we met face-to-face. She was just shy of celebrating her 100th birthday. Harriet followed her mother unexpectedly the following year.

More than 20 years have passed since we returned those letters to Lyndal. Except when the stacks of old dusty boxes begin trickling out onto the floor of my living room, I am mostly thankful for my husband's penchant for rescuing lost antiquities. He reunited three souls that day by returning the letters and photographs to their rightful owners, and we in turn received the friendship of two wonderful women we would have likely never known.

I am thankful for the way time speaks to my husband; I joke that he's never met an antique he didn't like. Hopefully, he will still like me, too, when I'm 100 years old.

INCARCERATED

www.girlfromgoatpastureroad.com – January 27, 2015

It's a matter of public record that my brother has been in and out of jail recently, charged with numerous offenses. Beyond the occasional speeding ticket, my brother's run-ins with the law and his subsequent incarcerations are a first for our mostly law-abiding family. It's a few hours' drive to visit him in the small county jail in the eastern part of the state where he is locked up. Beyond the drab municipal buildings and razor-wire fencing surrounding the courthouse, it's the kind of small town whose people have not enough to do and not enough resources to do it with.

Jail visits are surreal for those of us not behind bars. It's difficult to know what to say or do. The thoughts that pass through my mind as I prepare for our visit do not seem especially appropriate or helpful. What, I wonder, does one wear to look like the little sister of a man who would *not* break the law? I feel the need to make a good impression, as if I am a reflection of my brother's guilt or innocence. I thumb through my assortment of formless sweaters, omitting the black and white striped one for the obvious reason. I select, instead, an outfit of neutral, colorless tones that will not show soil or call too much attention.

Then my mind shifts from my wardrobe to that old familiar comfort of food. Shouldn't I bake a cake for the occasion? Folks always did that on the old television shows, right? I imagine myself explaining the presence of a pound cake to the guards: "I would not hide a weapon inside, honest officer, I wouldn't." I just think it would be so very nice to take my brother a cake so that he could share it with his cellmate and the guards. Maybe that would earn him some television time or a walk outside for some fresh air.

The Long Way Home

I ride down with two of my nephews, my brother's grown children. The three of us lead busy lives with our families and work — too much to do and not enough time to do it in. We stop to eat lunch at a local diner and I enjoy catching up with these men who used to be little boys. The youngest, Michael, says, "Aunt Susie, this would be fun if we didn't have to... "

He doesn't have to finish the sentence. I know what he means.

At the jail, my nephews and I huddle around one of three small windows just off the lobby. We attempt to speak with my brother via a menacing telephone that appears to be left over from the 1960s. I immediately regret not bringing antiseptic wipes and chastise myself for having had my mind on other foolish matters, like the outfit and the cake. The telephone line is filled with so much static that my brother sounds miles away instead of a mere two feet behind a panel of glass. What cannot be heard or spoken in words is evident in the setting of his jaw, the cold dullness of his blue eyes, and everyone's aching to get out of there.

Later, I make small talk with the guards. They laugh good-naturedly about my brother, who can be humorous and quite charming when he is not armed or had too much to drink. Even without the cake, I finally succeed in endearing the guards to please pass my brother a pair of my old reading glasses and a pen so that he can read and write. Along with adding a few dollars in his canteen, it is all I can offer: this weak but real connection to the outside world.

Still, I am angry at my brother, angry at his choices and actions. At times, I can barely contain it, and at times I do not. There is the feeling that he has brought an undesirable element to our lives and a fear that it might somehow be contagious. I want it to go away. I do not want our family poisoned. I miss the brother who I knew, my brother who is all but lost now from his family and friends. The numerous charges against him include assault, making threats, and discharging a firearm in the city limits. The real crime, however, is the life gone missing outside his jail cell.

He is my older brother by 15 years and I am the little sister who grew up believing that he hung the moon. One of my earliest memories of him is when I was three or four. I insisted on staying up past my bedtime to watch television. Each time daddy put me in bed, I would immediately crawl out. When my patient father finally threatened to give me a spanking, my brother met him in the hall. "Don't hit her, daddy. Don't hit her," he said, repeatedly slamming one fist into the other. I never did get a spanking that night, although I should have. I hold fast to this memory of my protective older brother. I would like to return the favor for him now but I cannot, and he won't listen. I have come to the hard realization that there is little I or anyone can do to protect him against himself.

My brother has always been a fighter, a trait that had rarely caused him any serious trouble until these last few years leading up to his incarceration. We're very different types of people, my brother and I. While he is a fighter, I am more of a flyer. Whereas fighters may appear tough with their inflated egos and an exaggerated sense of self-worth, the flyers among us tend to exhibit opposite characteristics. Flyers often forget to claim their own power and self- worth. These types of feelings can sit and ferment in your stomach, then eat you from the inside out; they skew our view of reality. They can make you lose sight of the many blessings in your life, causing them to feel as sparse as a path of breadcrumbs you dropped in the woods. Most days, I recognize these feelings as the negativities of life that for years I simply swallowed. As a child, this was how I knew to cope in the world, but now, I have come to wonder if maybe I don't deserve more. I have responsibilities to many, but most importantly to myself. Still, change is scary and I fear what could emerge if I loosened the lid on my own Pandora's box.

Sometimes, what seems to be the simplest thing to do can be the most difficult, can't it? To serve our time and walk away, when we are able, and free ourselves from whatever it is that imprisons us. Why is it so difficult to leave behind those old behaviors that are self-destructive and that no longer serve us well? It reminds me that we are all incarcerated, each in our own cell, searching for a means of escape.

FEARLESS

www.girlfromgoatpastureroad.com – January 5, 2014

Fearless. That's what a good friend called me recently. "Look at what you did this past year," she said. "You went up in a sailplane. You snorkeled over a shark. Sue, you're not afraid to try new things. You put yourself out there all the time. Oh, and remember that time you went hiking by yourself in the Alps and were almost mauled by wild goats?"

I had to laugh. If she didn't think I was afraid of those goats, she was dead wrong.

Several years ago, I traveled through Switzerland with my sister and brother-in-law. We took a cog train up the Pennine Alps along the Gornergrat ridge, one of the many tall peaks surrounding the famed Matterhorn. After completing our sightseeing, we boarded the train for our descent back to the village of Zermatt. The conductor announced that one of the upcoming stops featured a short hike to a glacial lake where the Matterhorn could be viewed in perfect reflection. Thinking of what a fabulous photo opportunity this would be, I assured my sister that I would be fine hiking across the open terrain, and so I fled the train alone.

With the great Matterhorn in front of me as a guide, I trekked the rolling green meadows with a Julie Andrews soundtrack playing in my head: "The hills are alive with the sound of music …" I meandered along zig-zagged paths that had been worn across the Alpine meadow, taking snapshots of colorful wildflowers and interesting lichens growing in the grass and on the rocks. During my close examination of the terrain, I also noticed some strange-looking pellets on the ground. Having seen no animals or wildlife along my hike, my curiosity was piqued as to what animal might have produced the scat. Placing a credit card on the ground for scale, I snapped a photograph of the pellets, intending to ask the guides about them when I reached the base of the mountain.

As I traipsed over each and every hill, I expected to find the lake on the other side, but instead I only found more hills. After a while, I began to get tired. I had been walking for a long time and the sun was shifting lower in the sky. I conceded that I was never going to find the lake. Discouraged, I turned around and began hiking back up the mountain in the general direction I'd come from. As I ascended the crest of a large hill that had been graded to accommodate the intersecting train tracks, I suddenly found myself standing face-to-face with a large herd of wild mountain goats, which were perched on a slight rocky ridge about 20 feet in front of me.

I quickly assessed the situation. I couldn't remember if anyone had ever been mauled by wild goats. I didn't think so, but I wasn't certain. I scanned the herd, where my eyes met the stare of a large, shaggy male standing in the midst of the others. His long horns curved like a sneer; he was obviously the leader. He stopped chewing grass long enough to size me up, a middle-age woman whose only possessions were the hiking clothes on her back, a credit card in her pocket, and a camera with numerous photos of mountains, wildflowers, and a ridiculous shot of goat scat.

There was nowhere for me to go except to try to get away. I backed up in as calm and nonthreatening a manner as possible. The herd shuffled nervously among each other. Panic began to ensue as babies bleated pitiful calls to their mothers. As the big male began to navigate the rocky bluff toward me on sure-footed hooves, the rest of the herd obediently followed. Then, with a toss of his head, he led the herd right past me, where they descended the mountain on the same trail I had come from. With my adrenaline pumping, I breathed a sigh of relief. I was safe.

I have been fortunate. Most of my life, I have only known fear in fleeting moments. Perhaps that is why I didn't recognize it when, years later, fear appeared to me in the form of anxiety. It would sit uncomfortably by my side for months on end. The more I tried to push it away, the more my efforts to resist only seemed to pull me further down. I was vaguely aware that something in my life wasn't working, but I wasn't sure what it was. I was 50 years old and felt exhausted. I felt like a machine going through the motions of life. It seemed like it took so much effort just keeping all the balls in the air. Some of the balls were mine, but I realized that many of the balls belonged to other people. I had simply picked them up as they rolled by and added them to my stack of things to feel responsible for. I had ignored my feelings for so long that I didn't know how to feel them anymore.

I felt broken, no longer able to pretend that everything was okay. Then, with that small act of surrender, the strangest thing happened. Immediately, I felt better. Imagine, allowing myself to feel broken actually made me feel better than trying to not feel broken. It was a revelation to me. I found I could no longer live in denial. The truth was revealed to me in the form of a question. What was I afraid of?

If I were to be honest, I would have to admit that I was afraid of so many things. I was afraid of dropping the balls. I was afraid of failure. I was afraid of being trapped in a life that didn't work for me. I was afraid of being found a fool, of handing over my power to other people, institutions, and circumstances that did not have my best interests in mind.

How I'd forgotten that simple feeling of being safe and cocooned by God's love! I'd forgotten that life itself calls us to step out in faith, not to withdraw. It took being broken for me to remember the truth that God is with us and within us all the time. I had to stop running and be still. I had to pause and breathe. As I began to relinquish control over people and situations that were causing my anxiety, they lost much of their power and influence over me. I was amazed to discover that I could let go and that miraculously, the sky would not fall.

RESURRECTION

www.girlfromgoatpastureroad.com – February 12, 2016

My husband, Perry, recently took full advantage of his state pension, retiring from the classroom to the sofa at age 51. "How can you stand going off to work each day knowing he's at home?" implored my friends. "He needs his rest," I conceded, remembering how he'd suffered a form of educational PTSD for several years post-retirement that caused him to break out in hives each September as the school buses began to roll.

After his retirement, I watched him unwind all right, almost all the way off his bobbin. He let himself go, wearing a threadbare path from our den to the refrigerator. In the evenings when I returned home from work, I often found him glued to the television set, attired in plaid polar fleece lounge pants and a sweatshirt bearing a trace of dribble around the neck. He washed whites with the coloreds and couldn't remember to get the recyclables to the curb without my nagging him. He played *Words with Friends*, most of whom he'd never met.

"Where - are - you?" Perry typed to an opponent in Paris or California.

"In - the - bathroom," I replied from across the hall.

An eternity seemed to pass before Perry mentioned that he was considering looking for a part-time job. Hallelujah! I saw the skies rip open and God's own hand reach down to retrieve a stack of overdue bills from my desk.

Week after week, he perused the want ads. It soon became apparent that no ordinary job would suffice. My husband wanted a flexible schedule, a low-stress job with people who wouldn't talk back or steal his stapler. Job security, maybe some benefits that didn't require him to don a fast-food uniform.

Life changed when he took a job at the funeral home.

Like Lazarus, Perry rose from the dead. He began to walk with a new kind of swagger, excelling in his new position while others were dying to get in. Muscles rippled beneath his starched shirt and black polyester suit from carrying around so much dead weight. Our neighbors nicknamed him "The Undertaker," and he wore his new title along with a brass nametag with glee.

Forget health insurance, this job came with benefits leading straight to the Promised Land. Complimentary burial! Discounts on cremation tchotchkes and commemorative afghans! For Christmas gifts to our nieces and nephews, we printed ourselves on chenille along with our birthdates and a dash that could be filled in upon our demise with a Sharpie.

As time went on, things began to get awkward between us as the line between reality and immortality began to blur. Whenever I misplaced my glasses, Perry would simply utter, "Sorry for your loss." For our 30th wedding anniversary, he sat me in the back of the car and surrounded me with a spray of white carnations. The last straw came after I slept in one Saturday morning and awoke to find a string tied around my big toe listing my name and date of birth.

Enough mortuary mayhem!

My husband had lost it and I had nearly lost him. I missed the old husband I knew and loved, even if he did come with a ring around the collar. His imprint had nearly disappeared from the sofa; the cushions had nearly returned to their original form. "Honey," I begged. "I miss you. I'd give it all back just to have you home again."

With that, my prayers were answered and the gates to the heavens clanged shut. My husband rushed toward me with his arms open wide; I shoved two piles of laundry into his outstretched arms and walked out the door to drop the recyclables off at the curb.

EPILOGUE: GLIMMER

www.girlfromgoatpastureroad.com – June 2, 2015

Feisty After 45, originally published as "Allegorie de soie," Elaine Ambrose, Ed.,
Mill Park Publishing – 2016

I rise before dawn and dress in the near dark. "You awake?" I call softly to my sister, a soft outline against the covers in the twin bed next to mine. I give her legs a gentle nudge.

Outside the open window, I hear *plink... plink... plink...* The previous night's rain leaks onto the dense vegetation below. Stepping up into the bathroom, I grope the walls for the light switch. Above the water basin, the bare bulb flickers awake. My sister Janie eases past me into the cramped bathroom and we quickly brush our teeth with bottled water. The bus is waiting.

The air outside is heavy and damp. Except for a handful of local outfitters and tourists who stumble toward the bus clutching coffee and backpacks, the outpost is still asleep. Along the street, seedy bars and overpriced restaurants sit idle and dark; souvenir stands cower under blankets of plastic. Wedged on a sliver of land between the Urubamba River and a sheer face of granite bolting straight from the earth, Aguas Calientes seems less like a town and more like a few forgotten crumbs lining the pocket of the giant Andes.

A loud *hiss* breaks the silence. With the release of the air brakes, the bus spasms to life and I lurch against my sister. The lights of the town vanish in the rain, drops of which trace solitary paths on the bus's windows.

It is January 2013. I can hardly believe that I am one week and 3,000 miles from home in the jungle surrounding Machu Picchu. My mind drifts back to the time leading to my departure. My husband was so upset with me for taking this trip that we barely spoke to each other. Was it my safety? Was it the money? The time I'd be away from home? I have never been entirely certain. When he gave an excuse for not driving me to the airport, my anger masked my hurt. Of course I could take a taxi; people did that all the time. I countered that since I could get myself to South America, I most assuredly could get myself to the airport.

He came through in the end, however, and insisted on seeing me to the gate. My departure was sullen, awkward. Was it too much to ask him to understand that I was drawn to this place like a divining rod to water? When our plane touched down in Peru, I still felt troubled and disappointed at what felt like a lack of support from the one person in my life whose approval mattered the most.

Our travels to this remote part of the world were made possible, in large part, by our mother who passed away peacefully in the wee hours of Christmas Day, 2009 after battling Alzheimer's disease and congestive heart failure. Throughout her illness, Janie and I had managed mother's care through funds located in a joint account. After mother's death, we contemplated what we should do with the remaining balance. Since our mom had loved to travel in her post-retirement years, we felt certain that she would have supported the idea of her daughters making memories traveling in her honor. We looked at a map of the world, assessed the remaining funds, and somehow ended up here.

Although the two of us had not worn matching outfits in 40 years, my sister had special shirts made for the trip: Carolina blue tees with a glittery typeface sprawled across our chests that read "Spending Our Inheritance." Wearing these shirts never failed to solicit a conversation about our colorful mother. Mom loved meeting people, and throughout her life, I don't think she ever met a stranger. It was apparent (especially when we wore those sparkling shirts) that her two daughters bore the same effect.

We were careful to arrange our trip with a reputable outfitter who specialized in small group adventure travel. We had hoped to escape the dreary weather back home, spending our time south of the equator basking in sunshine, the seasons reversed. Instead, we learned that in the highlands of Peru, there are just two seasons — wet and dry — and although the showers thus far had been sporadic and brief, we arrived at the height of the rain.

Constructed in the fifteenth century, Machu Picchu is located in a remote area of northern Peru, where the rugged Andes Mountains collide with the Amazon jungle; the humidity and altitude of this juxtaposition combine to create a stunning ecosystem called a cloud forest. Carved from a saddle of land that stretches between two mountain peaks, Huayna Picchu (Young Peak) and Machu Picchu (Old Peak), the archeological site of Machu Picchu is invisible from the valley floor below, encircled on three sides by a loop of canyon that falls over a thousand feet to the river. Originally thought to be a citadel, archeologists now believe that Machu Picchu was a religious sanctuary, observatory and royal estate for the Incan emperor Pachacutec.

The earliest trekkers to Machu Picchu would have travelled on foot for several days along the famed Inca Trail. In 1911, American explorer Hiram Bingham and his team of guides were exploring other Inca sites nearby when a local farmer tipped them off about an extensive set of ruins set high above the Urubamba River. Traveling in a steady downpour of rain, first by mule and then on foot, Bingham found the magnificent stone terraces and mortared walls of Machu Picchu barely visible beneath a thick layer of vines and bamboo thickets. Today, despite its designation as a UNESCO World Heritage site, modern transportation options, a century of improvements (a second access point was created from the valley below) and an ever-vigilant war to keep the jungle at bay, simply getting to Machu Picchu continues to take much planning and effort.

For most tourists, the gateway to Machu Picchu is the ancient city and former Inca capital of Cusco. At 11,000 feet above sea level, Cusco's Alejandro Velasco Astete International Airport ranks as one of the world's highest elevation airports. Visitors and residents alike in this area commonly become afflicted with a type of altitude-related sickness called soroche. Normally, symptoms range from relatively mild to flu-like, although if left untreated, soroche can become life-threatening. To minimize our chances of becoming ill, we arrived with our pre-filled prescriptions of Diamox and followed instructions to eat light meals, stay hydrated, and get plenty of rest.

The indigenous people here, on the other hand, have long looked to nature to ward off the symptoms of soroche. For thousands of years, leaves from the coca plant have been used in various ways to provide increased stamina and to help minimize the effects of the altitude. Before leaving the terminal, our guides served us a special hot tea made from this native herb. While coca is considered an illegal substance across many international borders (the leaves are combined with other ingredients and used in the production of cocaine), its consumption throughout the Andes is as vastly popular and culturally acceptable as sweet tea and tobacco here in the South. Coca tea is served in all hotels and restaurants. During hikes, guides always carry leaves for their groups to chew. In addition to medicinal use, coca leaves are considered sacred here and their usage permeates all sorts of cultural and religious activities.

After leaving Cusco and before heading to Machu Picchu, we spent several days acclimatizing in the lower altitudes of the Sacred Valley, exploring the small villages and archeological sites which comprise the heart, soul and fertile homeland of the Inca civilization. We sampled a good portion of the area's more than 4,000 native species of potatoes but due to a risk of contamination, were advised not to drink a single drop of its water. We dined on traditional foods like roasted guinea pigs, "cuy chactado"; ceviche; and washed it all down with pisco sours, Peru's national drink. Along the roadside, we noticed that many homes and establishments posted red flags beside their doors, an indication that within was a fresh batch of "chicha" — a popular beer made from corn — prepared and for sale.

To better understand the daily lives of the local culture, our guide, Juan, a native Peruvian, took us to meet a local family with whom he had befriended. We travelled far off the main roads, stopping in front of a simple two-story house. The house, the yard — everything — seemed to be made of brown dirt. A couple of handmade wooden ladders were propped against the second-floor windows; a cow was tethered along the grassy knoll beside the road.

We were greeted at the door by a short, solemn woman with a thick mane of glossy black hair. She was modestly attired in a long-sleeve cardigan, A-line skirt, and dark lace-up shoes. While she might have been in her early 30s, it was hard to tell for certain. A young child of perhaps five or six years old peered out at us from behind the folds of her skirt. After making pleasantries with Juan, the woman invited us to join her inside the house in small groups of three or four.

Stepping across the threshold was like walking back in time and it took a few moments for my eyes to adjust. Inside we found a dimly lit room that seemed to function as living room, dining room, and kitchen. A large earthen fireplace occupied the corner, surrounded by sparse stick-built furnishings, a wall-hanging, and several large, weathered pots. When the woman stooped to kindle the flames, I became startled by a motion of frenzied activity near my feet. Cuys (small guinea pigs) have long been considered both sacred and a delicacy in this part of the country. A dozen or so of the little critters ran wild about the room, squealing in tinny, high-pitched voices among the shadows and scattered bits of straw.

It was a relief to step back outside into the bright light and fresh air. Juan translated from the woman's native Kechuan that her husband and older children were at work this day, grazing their livestock in the distant pastures. For the first time, she smiled at us — there, was that a glimmer from a gold tooth? — and gestured toward numerous shapeless forms scattered across the yard and hanging from tree limbs. Upon closer inspection, I recognized several leather hides and animal carcasses, glass bottles, and wooden buckets, all covered by a thick layer of dust. These items, Juan explained, were relics of a celebration. After living with her husband for many years and bearing his family, they had recently married. Here, it is customary to marry only when one can afford a large celebration. It had taken them nearly 20 years to afford to marry.

This woman was proud of her home and she motioned for us to follow her to the back yard. She beamed as we admired the lush vegetable garden and a small paddock, where a scrawny goose and a few ducks squawked at each other across the dried mud. Juan explained that she had experienced some recent problems with erosion and directed our eyes toward the steep hillside 50 feet from her back door. Here, dozens of holes receded into the moist earth of the hill, tombs of Incan ancestors freshly looted by the spring rains.

Before departing, we presented to the woman and little boy small tokens of appreciation that we had brought from home:

coloring books and pencils for the children, gardening gloves, pottery and textiles from our native country for the woman. I created a small book for the family, which included maps and pictures of my native North Carolina and my family. I explained how I was traveling with my kanichu, my sister. Juan also presented her with a cash gift to which we had all contributed. She smiled again, seemingly touched by our generosity. The little boy's eyes sparkled with merriment. While clutching his new book, he played a little game of peek-a-boo with us, hiding behind his mother and then peering out at us from behind his long lashes.

As the bus pulled out of the yard, the boy waved to us goodbye. My formerly ebullient sister, a retired elementary school teacher, sat beside me, closest to the window. I watched her eyes fix on the child as she opened and closed her hands slowly in return. She flashed him her most beautiful smile, even as a tear wound its way down her cheek.

Our spirits were reeling with emotions, palpable, over the dull hum of the bus's engine. Sitting on the bus, halfway around the world from my middle-class American life, my worries seemed distant and small. I thought about what we had done to help this family and wondered if perhaps I shouldn't have done more. Sensing our discomfort, Juan explained that while it might seem to us that this family was very poor, they were in reality among the wealthier in the community, owning both a house and farmland. In the agricultural belt of the Sacred Valley, poverty does not usually equal the hunger that is so prevalent in many parts of the world. Here, it is more the poverty of a forgotten people — people forgotten by time and by opportunity. It is the poverty of a hardscrabble life and of hope clawed out of the dirt.

It was Mark Twain who observed "Travel is fatal to prejudice, narrow-mindedness and bigotry," and based on what I have seen of the world, I would have to agree. Travel, really intimate travel as opposed to the drive-by kind where one simply collects stamps on their passports or views the world from the isolation of their state room, permanently changes who we are and our relationship to the world. I suddenly realized that while I could not comprehend what day-to-day life was like for that woman, in the ways that mattered, we were exactly the same. While I could hardly comprehend the challenges of 500-year-old corpses washing from their graves into my backyard or having my dinner dwelling among my family on our living room floor, I knew for certain, in that moment, the absolute truth of our shared humanity. While the details of our journeys may be different, doesn't everyone want the same things in life? We want to experience both sides of love and to know that our lives go forward with meaning and purpose. We want, however small and tender, our morsels of dignity. That moment on the bus — for the first time in a long while — I felt alive and fully engaged, tapped into that God-like frequency of universal love.

Even in a developing country like Peru, everything is not ancient. There are cell phones and soccer balls, Coca-Cola and worn remnants of American clothing to be found if you look hard enough. Still, the unsteady march of progress into age-old traditions often yields ironic, if not humorous results that are not easily lost upon outsiders. When my sister fell and skinned her knee on the cobblestone streets of Písac, within a day or so, the cut became swollen and red. Juan predicted an infection and insisted that we seek medical treatment at the local hospital. He managed to procure us a taxi of sorts, which took us to a newly constructed building that, by Western standards, more accurately resembled a clinic than a hospital. Upon our entry, two professionally attired young ladies greeted us from behind the front desk; I noticed that the waiting area was immaculately clean. After admitting us into an examination room with a child-size exam table (or, we joked, for a very short Andean adult), the nurse confirmed that while the cut appeared to be infected, the hospital had no available medicines with which my sister could be treated. The hospital also, in a great irony, had no doctors. We were sent away with a fresh gauze wrap, thankful when, on the following day, a traveling doctor appeared at our hotel room with a fishing tackle box full of antibiotics.

In fact, before consulting a medical doctor, most of the population first seek a medicine man, or curandero, for healing, particularly if they believe their physical ailments stem from a spiritual one. In the highlands of rural Peru, this belief is deeply rooted in their culture. Curanderos practice, alongside their priestly counterparts, a form of hybrid Catholicism where personal shrines may contain — in addition to traditional candles, photos, and beads — the bones or mummified remains of ancestors and sacred animals. Here, the Virgin Mary bears an uncanny resemblance to the local Andean women in their colorful woven garments and bowler hats. After colonizing Peru, the Spanish forced the indigenous peoples to convert from their native forms of worship to Catholicism. As a result of this action, the worship of many Inca deities manifested themselves through their Catholic equivalents. The Virgin Mary, for example, became synonymous with the Inca's much-loved and benevolent mythological goddess, Pachamama, the spirit of Mother Earth.

When Juan informed us that he had arranged for us to attend a healing ceremony (called a despacho) with the area's curandero, we thought it was to heal my sister's leg. We were alarmed; we did not want to become involved with any sort of Incan "hocus pocus." Juan was merely teasing us; he explained that the purpose of a despacho ceremony was not to cure a specific ailment or illness, but, rather, to aid in the "dispatch" of our individual prayers to our own God.

For the ceremony, we traveled deep into the backcountry. Driving past the simple mud houses, we noticed an unusual ornamental feature. Nearly all rooftops bore a small cluster of ceramic bulls, along with any number of additional items ranging from crosses to bottles and Peruvian flags. Juan explained that this tradition was left over from the time of the Incas. While the bulls had long symbolized good luck, fertility, and protection, the additional items were a reflection of contemporary culture, alluding to the individual's particular beliefs and superstitions.

We pulled onto a grassy knoll on which sat a simple wooden shelter. In the distance was an unobstructed view of several mountain peaks. While the land looked much the same as the surrounding acreage, we were told that this was a sacred site that had been set aside for public use by the Incas. The shaman waited for us in the shade; his acknowledgement of us consisted of a simple nod. He was of middle-age, wearing modern clothes and black lace-up leather shoes beneath his traditional Andean clothing. I sat down beside my sister on the wooden bench. I couldn't help but think how our time in Peru had already been filled with so many unique experiences unlike any other. What could this experience possibly have in store?

Each of us was given three coca leaves. Juan showed us how to hold them like a fan, with the leaves branching out as if they had a common stem. Juan told us this was called a "k'intu," a symbol of earth, heaven, and the underworld. Reminiscent of the Christian trinity, I wondered if this symbol was another cultural hybrid, manifested from Spanish, Catholic, and Inca roots.

One by one, we stood before the curandero. Prior to beginning a despacho, participants must be spiritually cleansed; the curandero brushed the outermost edges of our bodies with a small brush, whisking away any negative energy. He unfolded a white cloth, spread it upon the ground, and began chanting softly. Onto this, he carefully placed a variety of objects, resembling a mandala. Juan explained the symbolic meaning of some of the items: shells, which represented the womb of the earth, and candies for the sweetness of life. To this he added an array of seemingly magical items, including flower petals, sparkling confetti, kernels of corn, herbs, and nuts. He added animal crackers, symbolizing our sacred relationship with the animal kingdom. Although the curandero remained stoic, we all nearly laughed when he topped it all off with a generous splash from a can of Bud Light. While Juan later explained that it was mostly a matter of convenience — the sealed and unopened can of was simply easier to transport than a glass jar of chicha — the sight of an Andean witch doctor presiding over a sacred ceremony with Bud Light defied translation. I could only surmise that like me, Pachamama sometimes needed a cold beer at the end of the day.

When it was time to offer up my prayers, I stood again before the curandero and tried to compose my thoughts. I gazed at the sacred view, across the low, fertile valley towards the rise of the distant Andes. Perhaps it was the calm demeanor of the curandero, or that any nervousness about the ceremony had been unfounded, but I was aware of a feeling of belonging and a solid connection to the earth; I didn't feel flighty as I often do. Then, in an instant, something (almost telepathically) flashed into my mind — both an intense gratitude for my time here and, simultaneously, an intense questioning of its purpose.

Why had I come here?

I realized then that I had no answer. With all the places in the world that my sister and I could have chosen to travel to, what had led us to this remote corner of the world? This revelation, posed in a question, was so basic, so startling, and so powerful, that I almost laughed out loud. *Why indeed had I come here?* I had traversed thousands of miles to this hallowed ground, eyes facing and feet planted squarely toward the spiritual world. Yet in my whole life, I have never felt so unsure of my direction.

I held my k'intu before me, closed my eyes, and with a deep breath, exhaled my litany heavenward.

The next day, we continued to Ollantaytambo, a small town whose proud heritage boasts a battle site commemorating a rare victory for the Incas over Pizarro's army. High above the town's cobblestone streets and walled terraces, the remnants of an ancient fortress guard a hillside temple and provide a stunning view across the landscape of the Sacred Valley. After fleeing the Spanish, many Incan families remained here, building and rebuilding their homes atop the original stone foundations. The town is laid out in neat organized squares just as it was then. Except for a small train station that sits near the edge of town, it retains, what I imagine to be, much of its original charm.

Today, Ollantaytambo is a jumping off point, the end of the road for nearly all travelers bound for Machu Picchu. From here, the terrain becomes impassable for automobiles; all travelers will either spend days hiking the Inca Trail on foot or will take the few hours' train ride into Aguas Calientes, a small outpost at the base of Machu Picchu.

My sister and I opt for the train, of course, wedging ourselves into the narrow seats that were obviously not designed for larger-scaled Westerners. Our carrier, Peru Rail, is not a luxury train, although there are several deluxe options available for those with more available funds than ours. We enjoy watching the scenery unfold as the train traces the winding path carved by the Urubamba River. We pass through the rich, expansive valley, shadowing terraced farmland, exposed archaeological ruins, and surviving portions of the rugged Inca Trail.

The train comes to a full stop at the edge of the jungle. This is not so much a gradual transition of the landscape as it is a living wall of green. As the engineer prepares for the final ascent into Aguas Calientes, our perception of space turns on end. Here, the landscape is vertical. Adorned with untold numbers of spiny bromeliads, tropical vegetation cascades like waterfalls down the mountainside. Compressed into the narrow chasm of the valley, the waters of the Urubamba have turned violent. The river thrashes into the canyon, spilling itself across boulders the size of automobiles. Buildings along the town's singular street hover on stilted foundations. I can only imagine that the flooding here is deadly and horrible.

As we exit the train, we see Juan and a second guide, Fernando, pacing nervously and glancing at the sky. A storm is moving in. After consulting the radio, it is decided that in order to beat the storm, we will skip the hotel check-in and immediately continue to Machu Picchu. Buses wait nearby to carry us straight up the mountain in a harrowing series of switchbacks. The route driving up is the same as the one going down, and when we meet oncoming buses, always on a straightaway, there are only inches to spare. Janie and I clutch the backs of our seats, afraid to look in either direction.

Half an hour later, we have arrived — without being killed —at the simple unadorned concrete entry gate to Machu Picchu. We walk through an antiquated turnstile and past a bronze bust of Hiram Bingham. We pass through a tunneled walkway, emerging on the other side of the mountain beneath a canopy of vegetation. The pathway leads us around an unsuspecting corner where we spill out into the light, blinded and senseless. There we find Machu Picchu, waiting, expecting us.

My jaw drops. I can hardly comprehend what my eyes are seeing; I am overcome with a sense of awe and wonder. Saddled on a sculpted ridge thousands of feet above the valley below, masses of clouds encircle the site, giving the illusion — or is it reality? — of a city suspended in midair. With the jungle kept at bay, the architecture appears to be a geometric series of precision-cut lines and angles — crisp stone blocks and clipped green terraces — while the distant peaks surround the site like moss-covered sentries. The storm has tinged the sky in a war of dark blue and purple while the clouds swirl and dance, looking for a place to rest. The stones, burnished and sun-soaked, seem to glow from within.

There is something magical about the light.

Since most of the other visitors have already left for the day, we wander relatively unencumbered, with the exception of the occasional free-range llama. While llamas are not native to this altitude, they have long been used by locals as domesticated pack animals. They roam the site at will, assisting the groundskeepers in maintaining the grass. Also present are strange rabbit-like creatures with short ears and long tails and whiskers. The viscachas like to sun on the rocks and make a great show of their annoyance by vanishing into the crevices as we approach. Entranced by these magical surroundings, we scale the labyrinth of stones and terraces while Juan explains Machu Picchu's history, legend, and lore.

Machu Picchu was designed as a self-sustaining and planned city. To the south, overlooking the river and following the contours of the mountainside, a great series of retaining walls were constructed to terrace the land for farming. These terraces had the capacity to support enough crops to feed thousands of people. To the north, more than 2,000 structures compose the urban sector, including residential, sacred and civic buildings, altars, fountains, and monuments.

Time and space were of the utmost importance to the Inca; sites were planned and structures designed to further enhance the Incas' relationships with both the celestial and natural worlds. Astronomy played a pivotal role in their cultural, religious, and daily lives. Machu Picchu is a natural observatory and possesses a remarkable alignment with the sun and stars. The site feels spiritually and physically protected by the sacred landmarks that surround it; the Apu (mountain spirits) encircle the site on all sides while the river seems to anchor it from below, holding it in a protective grasp. Although the Incas' complex religion incorporated the worship of many gods — polytheism — the most important was Inti (the sun god) whom they claimed as their ancestor and the source of their divine right to rule. They also believed in huaca, a religious concept where minor spirits may inhabit certain places, things, and even people.

As an agricultural society, the Incan religion provided them with practical guidance for seasonal activities such as planting and harvesting. One of the most sacred objects in Inca culture was the Intihuatana stone, which functioned much like a primitive celestial computer to calculate the equinox and to measure the angles of the sun for important celestial periods and events. Since these stones were of supreme significance, they were systematically sought and destroyed by the invading Spaniards. They were regarded as such a source of divine power that the Incas believed that breaking them would cause their resident deities to die or depart. Since the Spanish never discovered Machu Picchu, the spiritual power of its Intihuatana stone would have remained intact. A massive slab of white granite, "The Hitching Post of the Sun," Machu Picchu's Intihuatana stone, stands out as special among the muted grey rock of the other masonry structures.

Inca masonry is of such fine quality that it is all but impossible to replicate, even with today's modern tools and equipment. Stones fit together so perfectly that there is no need for mortar. Centuries of earthquakes and mudslides have had little effect on their stability. In fact, during earthquakes, it is said that the stones of Machu Picchu simply "dance," shifting with the motion of the earth before settling back into their original positions. While the wooden members and thatched roofs have decayed with time, the stonework remains in near perfect condition. Some researchers speculate that Machu Picchu may have still been under construction at the time of its abandonment. Juan directs our attention to a quarry sitting unobtrusively at the edge of the site, scattered with a plethora of partially carved stones. It appears as if one day, the city's occupants simply dropped their tools and vanished.

Understandably, the people of this region feel a certain amount of indignation at Bingham's claim of "discovering" Machu Picchu. Their ancestors, after all, had known of its existence for centuries and it is speculated that they may have never really left. In addition to the local farmer who led Bingham's expedition directly to the site, other families were living and farming here at the time of Bingham's arrival. While the final chapter in Incan history tells how the remaining Incas, including Manco Inca, retreated deep into the jungle to their final sanctuary, a settlement called Vilcabamba, it seems plausible that some of the residents would have stayed behind. Explorer Hiram Bingham would eventually become a U.S. senator, but at the time, he was an instructor in South American history at Yale University. His explorations were deemed credible and were largely underwritten by the university, who published his articles in *National Geographic* and brought Machu Picchu to the attention of the world. Bingham made subsequent visits to Machu Picchu, excavating the ruins and taking back with him thousands of artifacts, including human bones. After years of heated diplomatic battles between Peru, the U.S. government, and Yale, these items have only recently been returned to their homeland. The experiences of the indigenous people of the Sacred Valley region, at the hands of these worldlier institutions, have been less than exemplary. Their stories are just coming to light, as missing chapters in the world's history books.

The allure of Machu Picchu is heightened by its mystery. We may never fully understand its untold secrets. Machu Picchu is considered by many spiritual seekers to be one of the great spiritual centers of the world; pilgrims flock to the site each year by the hundreds of thousands. Machu Picchu calls to us across the centuries, as relevant today as it was in its heyday. It stands tall among mankind's greatest artistic and architectural achievements. Here, where heaven meets earth and human ambition meets fragility, we find, simply, that there are no easy answers.

※

The next morning, the sky dawns to a low grey ceiling. I plan to hike with a few members of our group to the Inti Punku, the Sun Gate, an area located 1,000 feet above the main site which marks the original entry to Machu Picchu from the Inca Trail. On rare mornings when the site is not shrouded in clouds, the sun is said to rise perfectly between its two large stones. Today, Janie will not join me on this outing. Her leg is bandaged and still sore from the infection. "Have fun and be safe," she calls. It is a testimony to the fact that as my older sister, she has long known and understood my penchant for alone time.

Before departing, our group joins Juan and Fernando for what has become a ritual when visiting the area's sacred sites. We hold our k'intus and say a brief prayer, paying respect to Pachamama and to the Apu. We set off, ascending the narrow trail that winds up the side of the mountain, thinning eventually to the rhythm of our individual paces. I have not gone far when I realize that I am still holding my coca leaves; impulsively, I slip a leaf into my mouth, biting into its green pulp. The flavor tastes bitter and I do not travel far before I spit it out.

I hold close to the mountainside, careful not to slip on the wet stones beneath my feet. Were it not for the Inca's highly advanced skills in engineering and road construction, this trail would have likely been washed away by a single storm. Portions of the old Inca Highway are still in use after more than four hundred years. Other than the sound of my own breath, it is perfectly silent. The clouds taunt and tease me, occasionally thinning into wisps of pale cotton candy. Beyond the trail, I glimpse a flash of blue sky; we have missed the sunrise.

I find that I am not disappointed.

I arrive at the summit where our other guide, Fernando, sits perched, his long legs thrown across a boulder like a spider. He is suspended by an invisible web, supported by stone and clouds. Lanky and handsome, he looks more Spanish than Kechuan. He has a surprising mouthful of silver braces and a self-conscious habit of lowering his head when he speaks. Chuckling to myself, I greet him by name. "Fernando" reminds me of the ABBA song of the same name, and I mentally hum a few bars. I pull my water bottle and some nuts from my backpack and sit down beside him.

"Your English is very good," I say. A faint smile emerges; he is pleased. He tells me how he grew up in Cusco. A few summers ago, he traveled to New York. He loves the U.S. and hopes to return when he has saved enough money. At the mention of home, I feel myself tense. A chill, from somewhere beyond the mountains, seems to blow right through me.

Without warning, Fernando suddenly stands, straightens his limbs, and descends from the boulder. With a parting word of caution, he disappears down the trail. I sit alone on the rock, arms curved around my knees, my thoughts confused by the sudden chill that rattled me a few moments before. What, if anything, had just happened? Had there been some cosmic shift — and had Fernando felt it, too? Or was it something internal — some sort of realignment confined to my spirit alone? Uncertain, I simply breathe. I inhale the vaporous clouds, the jungle's earthy scent. Staring into the abyss, I will myself to remember this exact place, this exact moment.

Along my descent, I discover that, in my absence, the jungle has come alive. Vines slither upward while orchids languish like jewels on emerald silk. A cacophony of trills and shrieks pierce the jungle canopy high above my head. In my peripheral vision, a glint of color — an apparition? — flashes just above the brush at the edge of the trail. I stop and peer up and then down. There is nothing there but clouds. I continue for a few yards only to see it reappear, this time hovering in midair like a glimmering orb. Small and transparent as cellophane, its color shifts from yellow to pink, lavender to silver. I try to snap its photo with my camera, however, the lens will not focus. Instead, it makes a hollow sound, moving in and out, as if nothing is there. A few more yards and, there! It reappears, flickering on and off for a few moments before disappearing into the mist. I rub my eyes and look again, but it is gone.

Am I imagining things? Is this the coca?

Suddenly, there is a break in the clouds. I forget about the apparition as the magnificence of Machu Picchu presents itself like a postcard far below me. The stone walls and terraces that I had walked among the previous day now appear cast upon the earth like forgotten puzzle pieces. I am humbled by the grandeur, the blatant excess of sheer beauty that I have been so fortunate to witness: a city in the sky.

Fernando is waiting at the trail's end. Our group scatters across the site, saying our goodbyes and snapping farewell photos. On the way back to the bus, I remember my encounter on the trail with the mysterious floating specter. I describe the experience to Fernando who listens intently. At first, he seems confused by my words until finally, his face widens and his braces gleam in the sunlight. "Ah, Sus-san," he says, enunciating my name in broken English. "There are many butterflies in the Amazon called morpho butterflies. They are very... umm, how do you say, *reflective.* Yes, they seem to change colors when they fly. That is it! You must have seen one on the mountain."

<hr />

A week later, I am back at home. I have returned to all my familiar comforts and yet, everything seems to be moving too fast. Here, I sleep in my own comfortable bed. I can go anywhere

I like, without fear of being washed off a mountain. There is an endless supply of fresh water from the faucet — I brush my teeth without using bottled water. I enjoy all the conveniences of a modern life, yet I find that I am filled with discontent. On nights I cannot sleep, I walk into my backyard. I look up to see the same sky that had held me pinned to those mountaintops. Now I feel weighted down by the earth. I believe that journeys have the power to change our lives but I wonder, for the moment, if it has been for the good. Somehow the "me" who left for South America a few short weeks ago does not feel like the same person who returned.

Although my encounter with the butterfly on the trail at Machu Picchu was quickly lost among the other memories and souvenirs from my journey, it was never entirely forgotten. The mysteries surrounding that experience piqued my curiosity and nagged at my consciousness like a splinter. Occasionally, my mind would drift back to Fernando's words about morpho butterflies and I would launch an impromptu search of the internet from my computer. Although I discovered many different types of morphos, none matched the same qualities of color and iridescence that I remembered. I learned that among the thousands of species of butterflies in the Amazon rainforest, new varieties are constantly being discovered (perhaps mine was a rare, undiscovered form of morpho?); I also learned that other species are constantly becoming extinct (what if it had ceased to exist?). Since these butterflies typically reside in the low-lying areas of the Amazon, how could I explain its presence — if it was not a figment of my imagination — at an altitude of nearly 9,000 feet? Given the innumerous species of butterflies in the jungle, including more than a hundred sub-species of morphos, I realized that I might never identify the one I remembered. If I never confirmed its existence, would I doubt myself forever and never fully believe that what I saw that day was real?

The Long Way Home

I finally came to believe that the creature I saw that day was not a coca-induced hallucination, but rather a morpho butterfly, just as Fernando had suggested. I first discovered my butterfly — *Morpho sulkowskyi* — not within the Internet's vast scientific Web pages, but, rather, in a painting by the artist Salvador Dali. Dali's *Allégorie de soie* ("Allegory of silk") was commissioned as a poster for the silk industry. The composition is a landscape of juxtaposing images: an oversize cocoon; an elegantly attired woman; and soaring among the other items, illuminated by crisp rays of light, are many unusual species of butterflies. The largest and most commanding butterfly, the one that caught my eye — is the *Morpho sulkowskyi*. The *Morpho sulkowskyi*, or the mother-of-pearl morpho is described as the world's most iridescent butterfly, with wings that shimmer like cellophane and reflect a shifting spectrum of colors like pale mirrored glass. When viewed from certain angles, it is said that the mother-of-pearl morpho can seem to disappear entirely.

As a designer and artist, my rediscovery of this mysterious butterfly in a painting seemed more than a coincidence; something about its message, from the trail to the canvas, seemed uniquely personal. While butterflies and cocoons are frequently used symbols of transformation, Dali presented his work in the form of an allegory to convey a deeper, hidden meaning. In Dali's altered reality, the woman is a representation of the potential of mankind's transformation, and the butterfly a symbol of the unique qualities present in all of us. I believe that we all possess the butterfly's diverse spectrum of color and light, the spirited and bright individuality. The butterflies in the painting soar interdependently across the brilliant light of the landscape; they remind me of the sisterhood of women who continually inspire and shape my life: my strong mother, my faithful sister, my beloved aunts and cousins, my amazing, wonderful friends. We are all morphos and painted ladies, swallowtails and monarchs.

This understanding of Dali's work revealed a deeper significance behind many of the seemingly disparate pieces surrounding my journey to Peru: the final gift from my mother, the support of my sister, the encounter with the shaman, the sense of a loss of purpose in my life, and of course the *Morpho sulkowskyi*. Through the lens of these experiences and the insights I gained on their behalf, I felt that the prayer I had blown across my k'intu that day in the sacred Peruvian field had been answered. I felt affirmed that my life was on its true and winding path.

I have come to believe that my sacred journey is a scenic loop. I move along with a sometimes faulty navigational system, at warp speed, a few hundred yards ahead of the marker on the road map. The points of reference are not always made clear to me, the driver. I must constantly remind myself to slow down and look carefully for the signposts, less I miss them altogether. Faith, something akin to intuition, tells me that they are there.

My time in Peru, a land that can take half a millennium to unearth its secrets, had a lasting and permanent effect on me. Like all journeys, it claimed a part of me as its own. It re-awakened my spiritual nature and reminded me that I must continue to acknowledge and cultivate those essential parts of myself that have long been forgotten or perhaps not yet remembered.

I have come to realize that I've not changed so much in more than fifty years: I am still the child my mother described as happy to spend hours playing alone, lost in thought and imagination. I'm still the country girl who grew up exploring roads that were so less traveled that they more accurately resembled rock paths. Despite the convenience of my current home in the city, the country is the type of place in the world where I feel most at home. I am a spiritual pilgrim, a seeker, and I am drawn, like a divining rod to water, to something larger than myself. I am simultaneously and inexplicably both a deeply satisfied and restless spirit. When

I cannot comprehend matters with my head, I find they are better understood with my heart.

It is disconcerting when we realize that we are living a life that no longer fits and yet, discomfort has always been a catalyst for change. The reality of metamorphosis is that it is uncomfortable; it bends and breaks us. I feel the pressure to grow and change is matched by a nearly identical pressure to stay in my cocoon and to shut out the light. To be less *Morpho sulkowskyi* and to be more of what the world wants me to be. It is a manifestation of the spiritual and our trust in the divine that leads us from these safe familiar places and down those unforged paths into the unfamiliar. As human beings, our journey is not so different from that of the butterfly. The only difference between the chrysalis, the caterpillar, and its final form — is time and space. Buoyed by the splendor, we find new places to soar. We glisten, we glimmer, we reflect the light that is all around us.

It was in the unfamiliar that I began to sense the stirrings of my own transformation.

And in the listening, I become alive.

ACKNOWLEDGMENTS

A heartfelt thank you to my family and friends for their love, support, and continued inspiration.

To my parents, Mary Louise and Clifton Swicegood, who taught me that I could do anything, including writing a book. A big hug to the world's best sister and my favorite traveling companion, Janie Sink, for being my number one fan. To my "other sister," Tracy Bauernfeind Forster, thank you for the times you are my memory.

I could never have written this without the Key West Girls Book Club, Angela Schlentz, Phyllis Little, and Lucia Kennerly. Thank you to Michael Lewis for his rad graphics skills and for washing the goat! To Susie Palmer, who was destined to become a part of this project, and to her mother, Toudie, who brought us all together and planted the seeds that became our home on Hill Street. Thank you, Joan Simpson and Linda Hedrick, for reading these stories and for laughing out loud more times than I can count. For my cousin Rene Smith, who dusted off her English-teacher skills to redline my mangled mess and for my editor, Katie Fennell, whose knowledge and expertise took this book to another level.

To my son Brennen, I love you to the moon and back.

And special thanks to my husband, Perry, for his patience during the many evenings I sat barricaded in my little room typing away on my laptop. Thank you for being the yin to my yang.

ABOUT THE AUTHOR

North Carolina born and bred, Susan Swicegood Boswell grew up in western Davidson County, down the road from her grandmother's farm on Goat Pasture Road.

A graduate of the University of North Carolina at Greensboro, she is a former blogger with *Skirt! Magazine* and is the author of the blog *Girl from Goat Pasture Road*. She has been featured numerous times on 88.5 WFDD's "Real People, Real Stories" and is a co-contributor to the women's anthology *Feisty After 45*. In 2014, her piece "Whippoorwill" was awarded Best Reader Memoir by *O.Henry Magazine*, followed by "Maples in October," which won second place for a work of fiction in 2015.

Susan lives in downtown Greensboro with her husband, Perry, and a menagerie of critters in what is technically an "empty nest," a 90-year-old cottage surrounded by huge magnolia trees, a backyard garden, and friendly ghosts.

Visit her blog at www.girlfromgoatpastureroad.com.